Aligning Purpose

Leadership's True North

Dr. Ty H. Wenglar, PhD

The Lionfish Press

5100 Long Arrow Canyon

Bee Cave, TX 78738

info@wenglargroup.com

Acknowledgments

To my parents, Buck and Lisa Wenglar and Sandi Richards, who planted the seeds of curiosity and love for learning in me. Thank you for teaching me the value of education and for being my constant source of motivation and encouragement.

In the loving memory of my grandmother, Myrtle "Totsie" Wenglar, whose support and belief in my potential were unwavering.

Dedication

To my beloved wife.

Cathy, you have been my rock, enduring the long hours and absences, managing our household, caring for our children with unwavering dedication, and ensuring our home was a place of peace and progress. Your ability to juggle countless responsibilities while being my steadfast supporter is nothing short of miraculous. I am forever grateful for your love, patience, and sacrifice.

Table of Contents

Acknowledgments   iii

Dedication   iv

About the Author   xii

Note to Readers   xiii

Foreword   xv

Chapter 1: Foundations and Principles of Purpose-Driven Leadership and Alignment   1

    Introduction   1

    Origins of Purpose-Driven Leadership   1

    Defining Characteristics of Purpose-Driven Leadership   2

    The Role of Purpose in Modern Business   3

    The Concept of Alignment   4

    Principles of Alignment   5

    Challenges to Alignment   6

    Strategies for Achieving Alignment   7

    Conclusion   10

    References   11

Chapter 2: The Power of Purpose in Leadership   12

    Introduction   12

    The Concept of Purpose-Driven Leadership   12

    Theoretical Frameworks for Purpose-Driven Leadership   13

Building Trust through Purpose-Driven Leadership 14

Driving Resilience through Purpose 15

Fostering Innovation through Purpose 17

The Impact of Purpose-Driven Leadership on Organizational
Performance 18

Sustaining Purpose-Driven Leadership 20

Conclusion 21

References 21

Chapter 3: Purpose and Strategic Alignment 23

Introduction 23

The Importance of Strategic Alignment 23

Theoretical Frameworks for Strategic Alignment 24

Integrating Purpose into Strategic Planning 25

Fostering a Culture of Alignment 26

Aligning Operations with Purpose 27

Leveraging Technology for Strategic Alignment 29

The Role of Leadership in Strategic Alignment 30

Measuring the Impact of Strategic Alignment 31

Sustaining Strategic Alignment 32

Conclusion 33

References 33

Chapter 4: Purpose-Driven Employee Engagement 35

Introduction 35

The Importance of Employee Engagement 35

The Role of Purpose in Employee Engagement 36

Theoretical Frameworks for Purpose-Driven Employee
Engagement 36

Strategies for Fostering Purpose-Driven Engagement 38

Leveraging Technology for Employee Engagement 39

The Impact of Purpose-Driven Engagement on Performance 40

Sustaining Purpose-Driven Engagement 41

Measuring the Impact of Purpose-Driven Engagement 43

Conclusion 44

References 44

Chapter 5: Purpose-Driven Innovation 45

Introduction 45

The Relationship Between Purpose and Innovation 45

Theoretical Frameworks for Purpose-Driven Innovation 46

Fostering a Culture of Innovation 47

Aligning Innovation with Sustainable Development Goals 48

Leveraging Technology for Purpose-Driven Innovation 49

Collaborating for Innovation 50

Building Resilient and Adaptable Organizations 51

The Role of Leadership in Purpose-Driven Innovation 52

Embedding Purpose-Driven Innovation into Strategy 53

Overcoming Barriers to Purpose-Driven Innovation 54

Measuring the Impact of Purpose-Driven Innovation 56

Conclusion 57

References 57

Chapter 6: Ethical Leadership and the Golden Rule 59

Introduction 59

The Foundations of Ethical Leadership 59

The Golden Rule in Leadership 60

The Role of Trust in Ethical Leadership 60

Empathy and Ethical Leadership 61

Ethical Decision-Making 62

Building an Ethical Culture 63

The Impact of Ethical Leadership on Employee Engagement 63

Fostering Inclusion and Equity 64

The Role of Corporate Social Responsibility 65

Sustaining Ethical Leadership 66

Conclusion 66

References 67

Chapter 7: Purpose-Driven Innovation 68

Introduction 68

The Relationship Between Purpose and Innovation 68

Theoretical Frameworks for Purpose-Driven Innovation 69

Fostering a Culture of Innovation 70

Aligning Innovation with Sustainable Development Goals 71

Leveraging Technology for Purpose-Driven Innovation 72

Collaborating for Innovation 73

Building Resilient and Adaptable Organizations 74

The Role of Leadership in Purpose-Driven Innovation 75

Embedding Purpose-Driven Innovation into Strategy   76

Overcoming Barriers to Purpose-Driven Innovation   78

Measuring the Impact of Purpose-Driven Innovation   79

Conclusion   80

References   80

Chapter 8: Purpose in Crisis Management   82

Introduction   82

The Nature of Crises and Their Impact on Organizations   82

The Role of Purpose in Crisis Management   83

Building a Crisis-Ready Culture   84

The Importance of Transparent Communication   85

Leveraging Purpose to Maintain Employee Morale   86

Adapting and Innovating During a Crisis   87

The Role of Corporate Social Responsibility in
Crisis Management   89

Learning and Growing from a Crisis   90

Sustaining Purpose-Driven Crisis Management   91

Conclusion   92

References   92

Chapter 9: Building Sustainable Success through Aligned Purpose   93

Introduction   93

The Concept of Sustainable Success   93

Strategic Alignment and Purpose   94

Engaging Stakeholders in Purpose-Driven Success   94

Fostering a Culture of Continuous Improvement   95

Leveraging Technology for Sustainable Success   96

Aligning Purpose with Environmental Sustainability   97

The Role of Ethical Leadership in Sustainable Success   98

Engaging Employees in Purpose-Driven Success   99

Measuring and Reporting on Sustainable Success   100

Building Resilient and Adaptable Organizations   101

Conclusion   101

References   102

Chapter 10: The Future of Aligned Leadership   103

Introduction   103

The Evolving Expectations of Stakeholders   103

Employees   103

Customers   104

Investors   104

Leveraging New Technologies for Aligned Leadership   106

Digital Transformation   106

Artificial Intelligence and Data Analytics   106

Blockchain Technology   107

Fostering a Culture of Continuous Learning   107

Lifelong Learning   107

Collaboration and Knowledge Sharing   108

Feedback and Reflection   108

Navigating Complexity and Change   109

Scenario Planning   109

Agility and Flexibility   109

Resilience Building   110

Embracing Diversity and Inclusion   111

Inclusive Leadership   111

Diverse Talent Development   111

Inclusive Culture   111

The Future of Sustainability and Purpose   112

Sustainable Innovation   112

Circular Economy   113

Conclusion   113

References   113

About the Author

Dr. Ty H. Wenglar is an accomplished construction executive and scholar in Organizational Leadership with extensive experience in multi-family development and construction. Renowned for his player-coach leadership style and a proactive, results-oriented mindset, Dr. Wenglar is actively involved in academic and community leadership roles. He has a passion for teaching, mentoring, and conducting research in leadership ethics and practices.

Dr. Wenglar's academic focus lies at the intersection of leadership ethics and organizational effectiveness, focusing on how foundational ethical principles such as the Golden Rule influence leadership styles across different cultural and organizational contexts. In his doctoral dissertation, "Exploring the Intersection of Ethical and Virtuous Leadership: An Analysis of Correlation and Interchangeability of Measurement Tools," Dr. Wenglar investigated the measurable impact of ethical and virtuous leadership traits on organizational outcomes.

Additionally, Dr. Wenglar's research delves into the application of ethical principles in leadership, seeking to enhance both theoretical and practical understanding of how aligning organizational purposes with ethical leadership can foster environments of compassion and integrity. Through his extensive experience and academic contributions, Dr. Wenglar continues to inspire leaders to embrace ethical practices and create positive, lasting impacts in their organizations and communities.

Note to Readers

Dear Reader,

Thank you for picking up this book on leadership. I want to address something you might notice right away: the book's size. This book is shorter than the industry average, about 25% shorter. You may wonder why, and I believe the reason is an essential part of what makes this book unique and, more importantly, valuable.

I do not consider myself a writer. I do not write for a living, nor do I aspire to become a full-time author. Instead, I write to share the knowledge and experiences I have accumulated over the last four decades. My journey has taken me from a common laborer to a corporate executive, from a lowly private in the U.S. Army to various roles in between. Along the way, I have earned an undergraduate degree, an MBA, and finally, a PhD in Organizational Leadership. Despite my academic achievements, I have never worked in academia, and I consider this a positive.

Many prestigious leadership scholars, though knowledgeable, often lack real-world experience. They might not fully understand the complexities and challenges that come with leadership in practical, everyday situations. My background is firmly rooted in the realities of the workplace, from the ground floor to the boardroom. This perspective allows me to provide practical advice and strategies that are immediately applicable.

The brevity of my book is intentional. I want to respect your time by getting straight to the point and providing you with actionable insights without the fluff. In the fast-paced world of business, I believe that concise, impactful information is more valuable than long-winded theoretical discussions. This book is designed to be read quickly, absorbed easily, and applied immediately.

Thank you for choosing to spend your valuable time with my work. I hope you find this book to be a useful and practical guide in your leadership journey.

Sincerely,

Dr. Ty H. Wenglar

Foreword

A couple of years ago, I broke my ankle. A simple slip while walking on a gravel incline resulted in a break, which within a week had escalated into a life-and-death situation when blood clots formed in both of my lungs. Today, I reflect on that experience with a profound sense of gratitude and insight.

Imagine, if you will, what I expected to be a mundane stay in a hospital bed under observation quickly morphing into what I can only describe as the scariest moments of my life. The sharp, consistent pain in my chest that had initially landed me in the hospital began to worsen. With my condition worsening very quickly, I came to a grim realization that I was fighting, with every ounce of my being, to grasp a simple breath of air. That night, in the deafening silence punctuated only by the frantic actions of a team of nurses, I feared I had lost that fight as I stopped breathing.

With that realization, I experienced fear unlike anything before or since then. The profound realization of being trapped within my own body, conscious yet unable to breathe, one of life's simplest acts, was terrifying. In those agonizing moments, even though the hospital room was a whirlwind of activity, the lack of oxygen (or maybe simply being scared s***less) began blurring my vision. As I was teetering on the brink of giving up, a grounding voice emerged, gentle yet determined, with one simple instruction: "Breathe."

Admittedly, my first thought was, what the hell do you think I am trying to do? But I realized that I was too consumed by all the distractions around me—the nurses, equipment, pain, and fear. So, I finally chose to filter out the external world, to latch onto that voice, letting it become my singular purpose, urging me to redirect and align every ounce of energy

I had toward the single purpose of drawing a breath. Against the odds, with that unwavering, singular focus, I managed to take a breath—faint but undeniable. From there, by maintaining that focus, things slowly improved, and a week later, I walked (okay, more like hobbled) out of the hospital.

Now, you may be saying to yourself, okay, that is a great story (or a lousy one), but what does any of it got to do with purpose, leadership, or any of the reasons you bought this book? Its relevance is simple: it is the profound lesson I learned about the incredible power of focus and alignment of purpose. My life that night depended on my ability to align my actions and mindset to a singular purpose—to breathe. Metaphorically, your success hinges on your respective commitment to aligning your efforts, goals, and processes, whether as an individual, team, or company, to a similarly singular purpose.

Working hard is admirable, but working smart with a unified purpose is transformative. The fact that you are reading this book illustrates the fact that you work both hard and smart as an individual. But this book is an opportunity to truly align your purpose, whether as an individual, team, department, or entire organization, synchronizing your efforts to achieve exceptional outcomes across all your projects.

This experience and the lesson it taught me about the power of focus and alignment are what I hope to impart to you through the pages of this book. By reading this book with a purpose, you can achieve remarkable success and create lasting value.

CHAPTER 1

Foundations and Principles of Purpose-Driven Leadership and Alignment

Introduction

Purpose-driven leadership and strategic alignment are foundational elements of organizational success. Purpose-driven leadership involves guiding an organization with a clear mission that transcends profit, focusing on social, environmental, and ethical considerations. Strategic alignment ensures that all individuals within the organization are working toward a common goal with a shared sense of purpose. This chapter explores the origins, defining characteristics, and importance of purpose-driven leadership and alignment, providing a comprehensive understanding of how these concepts can transform organizations and create lasting value.

Origins of Purpose-Driven Leadership

The origins of purpose-driven leadership can be traced back to early philosophical and ethical theories. Ancient philosophers such as Aristotle emphasized the importance of virtuous leadership, which focuses on the well-being of individuals and society. This notion of ethical leadership laid the groundwork for the modern concept of purpose-driven leadership.

In ancient civilizations, leaders were often seen as stewards of their communities, responsible for the welfare of their people and the environment. For example, Confucian philosophy in ancient China stressed the

1

importance of moral integrity and benevolence in leadership, principles that resonate with modern ideas of ethical and purpose-driven leadership.

In the 20th century, figures such as Mahatma Gandhi and Martin Luther King Jr. demonstrated purpose-driven leadership on a global stage, using their influence to drive social change and advocate for justice and equality. Their leadership was characterized by a deep commitment to a cause greater than themselves, inspiring millions to take collective action.

The business world began to formally recognize the importance of organizational purpose with the advent of corporate social responsibility (CSR) in the mid-20th century. Companies such as Johnson & Johnson, with its famous Credo, began to articulate their responsibilities to various stakeholders, including employees, customers, and communities. This era marked the beginning of businesses viewing their role in society beyond mere profit generation, aligning their operations with broader societal goals.

Defining Characteristics of Purpose-Driven Leadership

Purpose-driven leadership is characterized by several key attributes that distinguish it from traditional leadership approaches. These characteristics include a clear and compelling purpose, ethical behavior, a focus on stakeholder value, and a commitment to long-term impact.

1. **Clear and Compelling Purpose:** Purpose-driven leaders articulate a clear and inspiring mission that goes beyond profit. This purpose serves as a guiding star, aligning the organization's actions and decisions with its core values and long-term goals. A compelling purpose provides employees with a sense of meaning and direction, fostering engagement and motivation. For example, when Howard Schultz returned to Starbucks as CEO, he reinvigorated the company by re-emphasizing its mission to inspire and nurture the human spirit, which resonated deeply with both employees and customers.

2. **Ethical Behavior:** Purpose-driven leaders prioritize ethical behavior and integrity in all aspects of their leadership. They lead by

example, demonstrating honesty, transparency, and accountability. This ethical foundation builds trust and credibility, enhancing the leader's ability to inspire and influence others. Ethical leadership extends beyond personal integrity to include creating robust systems and processes that ensure ethical practices throughout the organization.

3. **Focus on Stakeholder Value:** Purpose-driven leaders recognize the importance of creating value for all stakeholders, not just shareholders. They consider the needs and interests of employees, customers, suppliers, and communities in their decision-making processes. This stakeholder-centric approach fosters loyalty, trust, and long-term relationships. Unilever's Sustainable Living Plan focuses not only on reducing the company's environmental footprint but also on improving the health and well-being of its stakeholders and enhancing livelihoods across its value chain.

4. **Commitment to Long-Term Impact:** Purpose-driven leaders prioritize long-term impact over short-term gains. They make strategic decisions that align with the organization's purpose and contribute to sustainable success. This long-term perspective ensures that the organization remains resilient and adaptable in a rapidly changing business environment. Purpose-driven leaders are often champions of sustainability and innovation; they understand that long-term success depends on the organization's ability to adapt and thrive in changing environments.

The Role of Purpose in Modern Business

In today's complex and dynamic business landscape, purpose-driven leadership has become increasingly important. Organizations face a multitude of challenges, including technological disruption, environmental sustainability, and social inequality. Purpose-driven leadership provides a framework for addressing these challenges and creating positive change.

Purpose-driven leadership enhances organizational performance by fostering a positive and inclusive culture. Employees who are aligned with the organization's purpose are more engaged, motivated, and committed to their work. This engagement drives higher levels of productivity, innovation, and customer satisfaction, contributing to the organization's overall success.

Moreover, purpose-driven leadership strengthens the organization's reputation and brand. Consumers and investors are increasingly seeking companies that demonstrate social and environmental responsibility. By aligning their actions with a clear purpose, organizations can build trust and loyalty among stakeholders, enhancing their competitive advantage.

Purpose-driven leadership is crucial in navigating the intricate web of modern business challenges such as the following:

- **Technological Disruption:** Purpose-driven leaders leverage technology to enhance their mission rather than just focusing on incremental profitability improvements. For example, Tesla's mission to accelerate the world's transition to sustainable energy guides its technological innovations in electric vehicles and renewable energy solutions.

- **Environmental Sustainability:** Companies such as Patagonia have made environmental stewardship a core part of their mission, influencing their product design, supply chain management, and corporate activism. This commitment not only addresses environmental challenges but also attracts customers who prioritize sustainability.

- **Social Inequality:** Purpose-driven businesses often engage in initiatives that promote social equity and inclusion. Ben & Jerry's, for instance, actively campaigns for social justice issues, aligning its business practices with broader societal goals and engaging its customer base in meaningful ways.

The Concept of Alignment

Alignment in an organization means that every action, decision, and behavior is in harmony with the overarching goals and values of the company. It ensures that all departments, teams, and individuals are moving in the same direction, working toward shared objectives.

When alignment is achieved, a powerful synergy is created that can propel the organization forward. Organizational alignment enhances productivity, fosters innovation, and builds a strong, cohesive culture. Alignment also makes it easier to navigate challenges and changes, as everyone is clear on the mission and their role in achieving it.

Alignment involves a continuous process of coordination and integration across various levels of the organization:

- **Strategic Alignment:** This process involves ensuring that the organization's strategic goals are in line with its purpose. For example, Google's strategic initiatives in artificial intelligence and cloud computing are closely aligned with its mission to organize the world's information and make it universally accessible and useful.

- **Operational Alignment:** Operational processes must support the strategic goals and the overall purpose of the organization. This alignment might involve optimizing supply chain processes to reduce environmental impact or ensuring that customer service practices reflect the company's commitment to customer satisfaction.

- **Cultural Alignment:** Organizational culture plays a crucial role in alignment. Leaders must cultivate a culture that reflects the company's values and mission. Cultural alignment may relate to hiring practices, performance management, and employee engagement initiatives that reinforce the desired cultural norms.

Principles of Alignment

1. **Unified Purpose:** A clear and compelling purpose provides direction and motivation. Leaders must articulate the organization's mission and ensure that it resonates with all members of the organization. This shared purpose aligns efforts and fosters a sense of belonging and commitment.

2. **Accountability and Standards:** Tom Landry's principle suggests, "You get what you demand. You encourage what you tolerate." Leaders must uphold high standards and hold team members accountable for their actions. Unaddressed misconduct can erode the fabric of the organization, leading to a decline in morale and performance. Establishing clear standards and consistently enforcing them is critical. Developing comprehensive performance metrics, regular reviews, and transparent disciplinary processes can contribute to accountable systems.

3. **Ethical Professionalism:** Upholding ethical standards is crucial for maintaining trust and integrity within the organization. Leaders must model ethical behavior and address any deviations swiftly. Sergeant Major Jason Broyles advised that failing to address unethical actions sets a dangerous precedent, implying that such behavior is acceptable. Promoting ethical professionalism requires a robust framework of policies and practices that uphold the organization's values.

Challenges to Alignment

Achieving and maintaining alignment is not without its challenges. Organizations often face internal and external pressures that can disrupt cohesion. Common challenges include the following:

1. **Inconsistent Communication:** Misalignment can occur when communication is inconsistent or unclear. Leaders must ensure that messages are conveyed effectively and all members understand their role in the organization's mission. Effective communication involves not just transmitting information but also ensuring that the message is understood and internalized.

2. **Resistance to Change:** Change can be unsettling, and resistance is natural. Leaders must address concerns and help individuals understand the benefits of aligning themselves with new strategies or initiatives. To manage resistance to change, leaders should involve employees in the change process, providing them with a sense of ownership and control.

3. **Diverse Perspectives:** Although diversity is a strength, it can also pose challenges to alignment if not managed effectively. Leaders should create an inclusive environment where diverse perspectives are valued and integrated into the overall strategy. Leveraging diverse perspectives requires creating a culture of inclusion where different viewpoints are not only welcomed but also actively sought out.

Strategies for Achieving Alignment

1. **Clear Communication:** Consistent and transparent communication is essential for alignment. Leaders should regularly share updates on goals, progress, and changes, ensuring that everyone is informed and engaged. Effective communication involves not only disseminating information but also creating opportunities for dialogue and feedback.

2. **Empowering Leadership:** Empowering leaders who can inspire and motivate their teams is crucial for alignment. These leaders model the organization's values, provide guidance, and foster a collaborative environment. Empowering leaders involves giving them the authority and resources they need to drive alignment within their teams.

3. **Continuous Feedback:** Regular feedback and open dialogue help maintain alignment by enabling leaders to address issues promptly and ensuring that everyone is on the same page. Leaders should create opportunities for feedback and act on it constructively. Feedback should be a two-way process where employees feel comfortable sharing their thoughts and leaders actively listen and respond.

4. **Training and Development:** Investing in training and development ensures that employees have the skills and knowledge needed to contribute to the organization's goals. Continuous learning fosters a culture of improvement and adaptability. Comprehensive

training and development programs should be aligned with the organization's purpose and strategic goals.

Case Studies: Purpose-Driven Leadership and Alignment

Ben & Jerry's: Purpose and Accountability

Ben & Jerry's, the iconic ice cream company, exemplifies the principles of purpose-driven leadership. The company's mission "to make the best ice cream in the nicest possible way" reflects its commitment to quality, social justice, and environmental sustainability (Ben & Jerry's, n.d.).

Ben & Jerry's founders integrated their social and environmental values into the company's business model from the beginning. The company's leaders prioritize ethical sourcing, fair trade practices, and environmental stewardship. Ben & Jerry's also engages in advocacy and activism, supporting causes such as climate action, LGBTQ+ rights, and racial justice.

By aligning its actions with its purpose, Ben & Jerry's has built a loyal customer base and a strong brand reputation. The company's commitment to social responsibility has also contributed to its financial success, demonstrating the power of purpose-driven leadership in creating long-term value.

Ben & Jerry's approach to purpose-driven leadership extends beyond its products and activism. The company's internal practices reflect its mission, with policies that support employee well-being and community engagement. For example, Ben & Jerry's offers extensive benefits and professional development opportunities to its employees, fostering a supportive and inclusive workplace culture.

Patagonia: Alignment and Sustainability

Patagonia, an outdoor apparel company, exemplifies alignment through its commitment to environmental sustainability. The company's mission, "to save our home planet," guides its strategic decisions, product development, and business practices (Patagonia, n.d.).

Patagonia aligns its operations with its purpose by using sustainable materials, promoting fair labor practices, and engaging in environmental activism. This alignment is reflected in its culture, where employees are encouraged to participate in sustainability initiatives and advocacy.

The company's leaders uphold high ethical standards and hold themselves and others accountable for their actions. This commitment to accountability and ethical behavior fosters trust and respect within the organization, contributing to its long-term success.

Patagonia's dedication to sustainability is evident in its innovative product designs and business practices. The company invests heavily in research and development to create environmentally friendly products, such as recyclable and organic materials. Patagonia's "Worn Wear" program encourages customers to repair and reuse their products, promoting a circular economy.

Interface: Sustainability and Innovation

Interface, a global manufacturer of modular flooring, exemplifies purpose-driven leadership through its commitment to sustainability and environmental responsibility. The company's mission "to lead industry to love the world" guides its strategic direction and operations (Interface, n.d.).

Interface's founder, Ray Anderson, embraced purpose-driven leadership after experiencing an "epiphany" about the environmental impact of the company's products. Anderson committed Interface to achieving "Mission Zero"—the goal of eliminating any negative environmental impact by 2020. This ambitious mission has driven Interface's innovation and sustainability initiatives, including the development of eco-friendly materials and processes.

Under Anderson's leadership, Interface transformed its business model to align with its purpose. The company invested in renewable energy, implemented closed-loop recycling systems, and collaborated with stakeholders to promote sustainability across the supply chain. By prioritizing purpose and sustainability, Interface has built a strong brand reputation and achieved significant financial success.

Interface's journey toward sustainability involves a comprehensive approach to environmental responsibility. The company continuously seeks new ways to reduce its carbon footprint and enhance the sustainability of its products. Its initiatives include innovative manufacturing processes that minimize waste and energy consumption.

Conclusion

Purpose-driven leadership and strategic alignment are essential for fostering a cohesive and motivated organization. By prioritizing a clear and compelling purpose, upholding high standards, and ensuring ethical behavior, leaders can create an environment that supports engagement, resilience, and innovation. Through real-world examples and practical strategies, this chapter has highlighted the critical role of purpose-driven leadership and alignment in transforming organizations and creating lasting value. By embracing these principles, leaders can ensure that their organizations thrive and contribute positively to society.

The integration of purpose-driven leadership and strategic alignment is not only a theoretical concept but also a practical necessity for modern organizations. As the business landscape continues to evolve, organizations that embrace these principles will be better equipped to navigate challenges and seize opportunities.

Leaders play a crucial role in embedding purpose and alignment into the fabric of their organizations. This approach requires a commitment to continuous learning, adaptability, and a willingness to challenge the status quo. By fostering a culture of purpose and alignment, leaders can inspire their teams, build trust with stakeholders, and drive sustainable success.

As we move forward, it is essential to remember that purpose-driven leadership and alignment are ongoing processes. They require dedication, reflection, and a proactive approach to address new challenges and opportunities. By staying true to these principles, organizations can create a lasting impact and achieve remarkable success.

References

Ben & Jerry's. (n.d.). Our Mission. https://www.benjerry.com/values

Interface. (n.d.). Mission Zero. https://www.interface.com/US/en-US/campaign/mission-zero-en_US

Patagonia. (n.d.). Mission Statement. https://www.patagonia.com/mission-statement/

CHAPTER 2

The Power of Purpose in Leadership

Introduction

Leadership is a critical component of organizational success, shaping vision, strategy, and culture. Purpose-driven leadership, which involves aligning personal and organizational values with a higher mission, has emerged as a powerful approach to inspire, engage, and drive performance. This chapter explores the concept of purpose-driven leadership, detailing how leaders can leverage purpose to foster trust, resilience, and innovation within their organizations. By examining theoretical frameworks, practical strategies, and real-world examples, we will understand how purpose-driven leadership can transform organizations and create lasting value.

The Concept of Purpose-Driven Leadership

Purpose-driven leadership involves guiding an organization with a clear sense of mission that goes beyond financial performance to include social, environmental, and ethical considerations. Leaders who embrace this approach prioritize the organization's purpose, aligning their actions and decisions with its values and long-term goals. Purpose-driven leadership fosters a sense of meaning and direction, inspiring employees to contribute their best efforts.

Purpose-driven leaders are characterized by their authenticity, integrity, and commitment to making a positive impact. They understand that their role extends beyond managing operations to include shaping the organization's identity and legacy. By connecting their personal values with the organization's purpose, they create a cohesive and motivating environment that drives engagement and performance.

Purpose-driven leadership is not only about having a vision but also about living it consistently. Leaders must embody the organization's values in their behavior, decision-making, and interactions with stakeholders. This authenticity builds trust and credibility, enhancing the leader's ability to inspire and influence others.

Theoretical Frameworks for Purpose-Driven Leadership

Several theoretical frameworks provide insights into the principles and practices of purpose-driven leadership. One such framework is Transformational Leadership, which emphasizes the role of leaders in inspiring and motivating followers to achieve higher levels of performance and personal growth (Bass & Riggio, 2006). Transformational leaders articulate a compelling vision, foster an environment of trust and respect, and encourage innovation and creativity.

Another relevant framework is Servant Leadership, which was proposed by Robert K. Greenleaf. Servant leaders prioritize the needs of their followers, empowering them to grow and succeed (Greenleaf, 1977). This approach aligns closely with purpose-driven leadership, as it emphasizes the importance of service, empathy, and ethical behavior.

Purpose-driven leadership also aligns with the concept of Authentic Leadership, which focuses on the importance of self-awareness, transparency, and ethical conduct (George, 2003). Authentic leaders are true to their values and principles, creating a trusting culture and a reliable leadership style that fosters loyalty and commitment among followers.

Case Study: Microsoft under Satya Nadella

Satya Nadella's leadership at Microsoft exemplifies the principles of purpose-driven leadership. Since becoming CEO in 2014, Nadella has articulated a clear mission "to empower every person and every organization on the planet to achieve more" (Microsoft, n.d.). This purpose has guided

Microsoft's strategic direction, fostering a culture of innovation, inclusivity, and customer-centricity.

Nadella's emphasis on empathy and continuous learning has transformed Microsoft's organizational culture. He encourages employees to embrace a growth mindset, focusing on learning and development rather than fixed achievements. This approach has revitalized Microsoft's innovation capabilities and strengthened its competitive position in the technology industry.

The CEO's purpose-driven leadership is also evident in Microsoft's commitment to social responsibility and sustainability. The company has set ambitious goals to reduce its carbon footprint, promote diversity and inclusion, and enhance digital access for underserved communities. By aligning Microsoft's purpose with its strategic objectives, Nadella has created a cohesive and inspiring vision that drives performance and engagement.

Under Nadella's leadership, Microsoft has also focused on developing products and services that align with its mission. Microsoft has invested in cloud computing, artificial intelligence, and other technologies that empower organizations and individuals to achieve more. This alignment between purpose and innovation has contributed to Microsoft's sustained growth and market leadership.

Building Trust through Purpose-Driven Leadership

Trust is a cornerstone of effective leadership, influencing employee engagement, collaboration, and organizational performance. Purpose-driven leaders build trust by demonstrating authenticity, integrity, and a genuine commitment to the organization's mission. They communicate transparently, act consistently with their values, and prioritize the well-being of the employees and stakeholders.

Building trust involves creating an environment where employees feel valued, respected, and supported. Purpose-driven leaders listen actively, provide constructive feedback, and recognize employees' contributions.

They also foster a culture of openness and psychological safety, encouraging employees to voice their ideas and concerns without fear of retribution.

Trust is also built through accountability and fairness. Purpose-driven leaders hold themselves and others accountable for their actions, ensuring that decisions are made ethically and transparently. They promote fairness and equity in all aspects of the organization, from resource allocation to performance evaluation, reinforcing the organization's values and purpose.

Case Study: Patagonia

Patagonia, an outdoor apparel company, is renowned for its commitment to environmental sustainability and ethical business practices. The company's purpose, "to save our home planet," guides its leadership approach and strategic decisions (Patagonia, n.d.). Patagonia's leaders build trust by aligning their actions with the company's mission, demonstrating their genuine commitment to environmental stewardship and social responsibility.

Patagonia's transparent communication and ethical practices foster trust with employees, customers, and other stakeholders. The company's leaders regularly share updates on its environmental initiatives, financial performance, and social impact, ensuring that stakeholders are informed and engaged. By prioritizing purpose and trust, Patagonia has built a loyal and motivated workforce, as well as a strong and reputable brand.

Patagonia's leadership also emphasizes the importance of employee well-being and development. The company offers extensive benefits and support for employees, including on-site childcare, flexible work arrangements, and opportunities for professional growth. This focus on employee well-being enhances trust and engagement, contributing to Patagonia's overall success.

Driving Resilience through Purpose

Resilience is the ability to adapt and thrive in the face of challenges and adversity. Purpose-driven leaders foster resilience by providing a clear sense of direction and meaning, helping employees navigate uncertainty with confidence and determination. A strong sense of purpose acts as a stabilizing force, guiding decision-making and actions during crises.

Purpose-driven leaders promote resilience by encouraging a growth mindset and fostering a culture of learning and innovation. They support employees in developing new skills, experimenting with new ideas, and learning from past failures. The adaptability and willingness to embrace change enhance the organization's ability to respond to evolving circumstances and seize new opportunities.

Resilience is also built through strong relationships and social support. Purpose-driven leaders cultivate a sense of community and collaboration, encouraging employees to support one another and work together toward common goals. This sense of belonging and mutual support strengthens the organization's collective resilience.

Case Study: Unilever

Unilever's commitment to sustainability and social responsibility is central to its purpose-driven leadership approach. The company's purpose "to make sustainable living commonplace" guides its strategy and operations, promoting resilience and adaptability in a rapidly changing market (Unilever, n.d.).

Unilever's leaders foster resilience by integrating sustainability into the company's business model and product innovation. The company, in its Sustainable Living Plan, outlines ambitious goals for reducing environmental impact, improving health and well-being, and enhancing livelihoods. By aligning its purpose with its strategic objectives, Unilever ensures that its activities create long-term value and contribute to societal and environmental resilience.

Unilever's focus on resilience is also reflected in its supply chain practices. The company works closely with suppliers to promote sustainable and ethical sourcing, enhancing the resilience of its supply chain. This commitment to sustainability and social responsibility strengthens Unilever's reputation and builds trust with consumers, contributing to its long-term success.

Unilever's leadership also emphasizes the importance of continuous improvement and innovation. The company invests in research and development to create sustainable products and solutions, fostering a culture of innovation and resilience. This forward-looking approach helps Unilever stay ahead of market trends and adapt to changing consumer preferences.

Fostering Innovation through Purpose

Innovation is a key driver of organizational success that enables companies to develop new products, services, and processes that create value. Purpose-driven leaders foster innovation by providing a clear sense of direction and inspiring employees to think creatively and take risks. A strong sense of purpose encourages employees to explore new ideas and solutions that align with the organization's mission.

Purpose-driven leaders create an environment that supports innovation by providing resources, support, and autonomy. They encourage employees to experiment, learn from failures, and iterate on their ideas. This culture of experimentation and continuous improvement enhances the organization's ability to innovate and stay competitive.

Collaboration is also essential for innovation. Purpose-driven leaders promote cross-functional collaboration and knowledge sharing, enabling employees to leverage diverse perspectives and expertise. They create opportunities for employees to work together on innovation projects, fostering a sense of community and shared purpose.

Case Study: Google

Google's mission "to organize the world's information and make it universally accessible and useful" drives its innovation efforts (Google, n.d.). The company's leaders foster a culture of purpose-driven innovation by providing employees with the resources and autonomy to explore new ideas and develop groundbreaking solutions.

Google's "20% time" policy, which allows employees to spend 20% of their work hours on projects they are passionate about, exemplifies the company's commitment to innovation. This policy has led to the development of successful products such as Gmail and Google Maps. By aligning its innovation efforts with its purpose, Google has built a reputation as a leading innovator in the technology industry.

Google's leaders also promote collaboration and knowledge sharing through initiatives such as "Google X," the company's innovation lab. Google X encourages employees to pursue ambitious "moonshot" projects that have the potential to create transformative change. This focus on purpose-driven innovation has enabled Google to develop cutting-edge technologies and maintain its competitive edge.

Google's approach to fostering innovation is also reflected in its commitment to continuous learning and development. The company offers extensive training programs and resources for employees to develop their skills and stay ahead of industry trends. This focus on learning and growth enhances Google's ability to innovate and adapt to changing market conditions.

The Impact of Purpose-Driven Leadership on Organizational Performance

Purpose-driven leadership has a profound impact on organizational performance. Research shows that organizations led by purpose-driven leaders tend to have higher levels of employee engagement, customer satisfaction, and financial performance. Purpose-driven leadership fosters a positive work environment, enhances trust and loyalty, and drives sustainable success.

Employees in organizations with purpose-driven leadership are more likely to feel valued, respected, and motivated. As a result, they report higher levels of job satisfaction, commitment, and productivity. Purpose-driven leaders also attract and retain top talent, as employees are drawn to organizations that are aligned with their values.

Customers are more likely to trust and support organizations that demonstrate purpose-driven leadership. Purpose-driven leadership enhances brand reputation and customer loyalty, leading to increased sales and market share. Additionally, purpose-driven leadership reduces the risk of costly legal issues and reputational damage, contributing to long-term financial stability.

Purpose-driven leadership also promotes innovation and collaboration. Employees in purpose-driven organizations are more willing to share ideas, take risks, and work together to achieve common goals. This culture of trust and mutual respect drives creativity and continuous improvement, enhancing organizational performance and competitive advantage.

Case Study: Starbucks

Starbucks' mission "to inspire and nurture the human spirit – one person, one cup, and one neighborhood at a time" guides its leadership approach and strategic decisions (Starbucks, n.d.). Its leaders prioritize creating a positive and inclusive work environment that aligns with this mission.

The company's commitment to purpose-driven leadership is reflected in its extensive employee benefits and development programs. Starbucks offers comprehensive health benefits, tuition reimbursement, and opportunities for career growth. This focus on employee well-being and development enhances engagement and performance, contributing to Starbucks' long-term success.

Starbucks' leaders also emphasize the importance of social responsibility and sustainability. The company's initiatives, such as ethical sourcing, environmental stewardship, and community involvement, align with its mission and create value for its stakeholders. By demonstrating purpose-driven leadership, Starbucks has built a loyal and motivated workforce, as well as a strong and reputable brand.

The company's leadership approach also includes a focus on continuous improvement and innovation. Starbucks invests in research and development to create new products and enhance the customer experience. This focus on innovation, which is aligned with its mission, helps Starbucks stay ahead of market trends and maintain its competitive edge.

Sustaining Purpose-Driven Leadership

Sustaining purpose-driven leadership requires ongoing commitment and effort from leaders. It involves continuously reinforcing the organization's purpose, providing support and resources, and adapting to changing circumstances while staying true to the organization's values.

Leaders should regularly revisit and reaffirm the organization's purpose, ensuring that it remains relevant and inspiring. They should also recognize and reward employees who demonstrate purpose-driven behavior, reinforcing the importance of purpose-driven leadership.

Sustaining purpose-driven leadership involves creating a culture of continuous improvement, where employees are encouraged to provide feedback and contribute to organizational success. Leaders should be open to new ideas and willing to adapt their strategies to better align with the organization's purpose and goals.

Case Study: The Body Shop

The Body Shop's commitment to purpose-driven leadership is reflected in its mission "to fight for a fairer and more beautiful world" (The Body Shop, n.d.). The company's leaders prioritize creating a work environment that aligns with this mission and fosters purpose-driven leadership.

This company sustains purpose-driven leadership by involving employees in its social and environmental initiatives. The company encourages employees to participate in activism and volunteer activities, providing paid time off for these efforts. This alignment with the company's purpose enhances employee satisfaction and motivation.

The Body Shop's focus on transparency and open communication further supports purpose-driven leadership. The company regularly shares updates on its social and environmental impact, ensuring that employees feel informed and connected to the organization's mission. By sustaining purpose-driven leadership, The Body Shop has built a motivated and committed workforce that drives its long-term success.

The company's commitment to sustainability and social responsibility is also reflected in its product development and sourcing practices. The Body Shop prioritizes cruelty-free and sustainable ingredients, working closely with suppliers to ensure ethical standards are met. This alignment enhances The Body Shop's brand reputation and customer loyalty.

Conclusion

Purpose-driven leadership is essential for fostering a positive organizational culture, building trust, and ensuring long-term success. By prioritizing the organizational purpose and aligning their actions with the organization's mission, leaders can create a cohesive and motivating environment that drives engagement, resilience, and innovation. Through real-world examples and practical strategies, this chapter has highlighted the critical role of purpose-driven leadership in transforming organizations and creating lasting value. By sustaining purpose-driven leadership and measuring its impact, leaders can ensure that their organizations thrive and contribute positively to society.

References

Bass, B. M., & Riggio, R. E. (2006). Transformational leadership. Psychology Press.

George, B. (2003). Authentic leadership: Rediscovering the secrets to creating lasting value. John Wiley & Sons.

Google. (n.d.). About Google. https://about.google/

Greenleaf, R. K. (1977). Servant leadership: A journey into the nature of legitimate power and greatness. Paulist Press.

Microsoft. (n.d.). About Microsoft. https://www.microsoft.com/en-us/about

Patagonia. (n.d.). Mission Statement. https://www.patagonia.com/mission-statement/

Starbucks. (n.d.). Our Mission and Values. https://www.starbucks.com/about-us/company-information/mission-statement

The Body Shop. (n.d.). Our Commitment. https://www.thebodyshop.com/en-us/about-us/a/a00005

Unilever. (n.d.). Sustainable Living. https://www.unilever.com/sustainable-living/

CHAPTER 3

Purpose and Strategic Alignment

Introduction

Strategic alignment is essential for ensuring that an organization's activities and goals are in harmony with its overarching purpose. An organization's purpose that is clearly defined and integrated into its strategy provides a unified direction that guides decision-making, resource allocation, and performance measurement. This chapter explores the concept of strategic alignment, detailing how organizations can align their purpose with their strategic objectives to drive sustainable success. By examining theoretical frameworks, practical strategies, and real-world examples, we will understand how aligning purpose with strategy can transform organizations and create lasting value.

The Importance of Strategic Alignment

Strategic alignment involves ensuring that an organization's goals, strategies, and actions are consistent with its purpose. This alignment provides a clear roadmap for achieving long-term success, guiding decision-making and resource allocation. An organizational purpose that is embedded into its strategy helps maintain focus and coherence, even as the organization navigates complex and changing environments.

Strategic alignment ensures that all parts of the organization are working toward common goals. The alignment of strategy fosters a sense of unity and direction, enhancing coordination and collaboration across departments. This coherence enables the organization to respond effectively to challenges and opportunities, driving performance and long-term success.

Organizations with strong strategic alignment are better positioned to achieve their goals and deliver value to stakeholders. The alignment helps ensure that resources are used efficiently and efforts are focused on activities that support the organization's mission. Strategic alignment also enhances the organization's ability to adapt to change, as a clear sense of purpose provides a stable foundation for decision-making.

Theoretical Frameworks for Strategic Alignment

Several theoretical frameworks provide insights into how organizations can achieve strategic alignment. One such framework is the Balanced Scorecard (BSC), developed by Kaplan and Norton (1996). The BSC provides a comprehensive approach to performance measurement, incorporating financial, customer, internal process, and learning and growth perspectives. By linking these perspectives to the organization's purpose and strategy, the BSC helps ensure alignment and coherence.

Another relevant framework is the Strategic Alignment Model (SAM), proposed by Henderson and Venkatraman (1993). SAM emphasizes the alignment of business strategy and IT strategy, highlighting the importance of integrating different aspects of the organization to achieve strategic coherence. This model can be extended to include alignment between the organization's purpose and its overall strategy.

Purpose-driven strategic alignment also reflects the concept of "Strategic Fit," which emphasizes the importance of aligning the organization's internal capabilities with external opportunities and threats. This alignment is achieved by continuously assessing and adjusting the organization's strategy to ensure that it remains relevant and effective in achieving its purpose.

Case Study: Patagonia

Patagonia, an outdoor apparel company, exemplifies purpose-driven strategic alignment. The company's mission "to build the best product, cause no unnecessary harm, use business to inspire and implement solutions to the environmental crisis" guides its strategic objectives (Patagonia, n.d.). This purpose is integrated into all aspects of Patagonia's business, from product design to supply chain management.

The company's strategic alignment is evident in its commitment to environmental sustainability. Patagonia invests in sustainable materials, promotes fair labor practices, and supports environmental activism. The company's "Worn Wear" program, which encourages customers to repair and reuse products, aligns with its purpose and strategic goals. By embedding its purpose into its strategy, Patagonia has built a strong brand reputation and achieved long-term success.

Patagonia's approach to strategic alignment also includes engaging stakeholders in its mission. The company collaborates with environmental organizations, participates in advocacy campaigns, and involves employees in sustainability initiatives. This holistic approach ensures that Patagonia's strategy aligns with its purpose and creates value for all stakeholders.

Integrating Purpose into Strategic Planning

Integrating purpose into strategic planning involves aligning the organization's mission, vision, and values with its strategic objectives. This process begins with clearly defining the organization's purpose and then communicating it effectively to all stakeholders. Leaders must ensure that the purpose is reflected in the organization's strategic goals, initiatives, and performance metrics.

One effective approach is to use the BSC to link the organization's purpose with its strategic objectives. This process involves identifying key performance indicators (KPIs) that reflect the organization's purpose and tracking progress toward these goals. Regularly reviewing and adjusting the strategy based on feedback and changing circumstances ensures that the organization remains aligned with its purpose.

Strategic planning also involves engaging employees and other stakeholders in defining and refining the organization's purpose and strategy. This participatory approach ensures that the purpose resonates with stakeholders and reflects their values and aspirations. Strategic planning also fosters a sense of ownership and commitment, enhancing alignment and engagement.

Case Study: Unilever

Unilever's Sustainable Living Plan demonstrates how purpose can be integrated into strategic planning. The Plan focuses on improving health and well-being, reducing environmental impact, and enhancing livelihoods, aligning with Unilever's purpose of making sustainable living commonplace (Unilever, n.d.).

The company's strategic planning process involves setting ambitious sustainability goals and integrating them into its business strategy. For example, the company aims to halve its environmental footprint, improve the health and well-being of a billion people, and enhance the livelihoods of millions. By linking its purpose with its strategic objectives, Unilever ensures that its business activities create value for society and the environment.

Unilever's commitment to strategic alignment is also reflected in its performance management system. The company tracks progress toward its sustainability goals using a comprehensive set of KPIs and regularly reports on its achievements. This transparency and accountability help ensure that Unilever's strategy remains aligned with its purpose and drives continuous improvement.

Fostering a Culture of Alignment

Creating a culture of alignment involves embedding the organization's purpose into its values, behaviors, and practices. Leaders play a critical role in fostering this culture by modeling aligned behaviors, communicating the purpose consistently, and reinforcing alignment through policies and practices.

One effective strategy for fostering a culture of alignment is to integrate the organization's purpose into its recruitment, onboarding, and training processes. This approach ensures that new employees understand and embrace the organization's mission from the outset. Regular training and development programs can reinforce the importance of alignment and provide employees with the skills and knowledge they need to contribute to the organization's strategic goals.

Leaders can also foster a culture of alignment by recognizing and rewarding behaviors that reflect the organization's purpose. This strategy involves setting clear expectations, providing regular feedback, and celebrating achievements that align with the organization's mission. By creating an environment where alignment is valued and rewarded, leaders can enhance engagement and performance.

Case Study: Zappos

Zappos, an online shoe and clothing retailer, is known for its strong culture of alignment. The company's purpose "to deliver happiness to customers, employees, and vendors" guides its business practices and strategic objectives (Zappos, n.d.).

The company fosters a culture of alignment by integrating its purpose into all aspects of its operations. Zappos' unique onboarding process includes a culture-fit interview and a $2,000 offer to quit, ensuring that new hires align with its values. The company also offers extensive training and development programs, emphasizing the importance of alignment and customer service.

Zappos' commitment to alignment is reflected in its performance management system. The company recognizes and rewards employees who demonstrate behaviors that align with its purpose, reinforcing the importance of alignment. This approach has helped Zappos build a highly engaged and motivated workforce, driving its long-term success.

Aligning Operations with Purpose

Aligning operations with purpose involves integrating the organization's mission into its day-to-day activities and processes. This alignment includes ensuring that products, services, and customer interactions reflect the organization's values and goals. Leaders must identify opportunities to embed the organization's purpose into the operational decisions, resource allocation, and performance measurement in the company.

One effective approach is to develop purpose-driven policies and procedures that guide operational decisions. This strategy includes setting standards for ethical sourcing, sustainability, and customer service that align with the organization's mission. Regularly reviewing and adjusting these policies ensures that operations remain aligned with the organization's purpose.

Leaders can also leverage technology and data analytics to enhance operational alignment. This approach involves using digital tools to track performance, gather feedback, and identify areas for improvement. By aligning operations with purpose, organizations can enhance efficiency, customer satisfaction, and overall performance.

Case Study: IKEA

IKEA's purpose "to create a better everyday life for many people" guides its operational decisions and activities (IKEA, n.d.). This purpose is reflected in IKEA's commitment to affordability, quality, and sustainability.

IKEA aligns its operations with its purpose by investing in sustainable materials, promoting energy efficiency, and reducing waste. The company's "People & Planet Positive" strategy outlines its goals for renewable energy, sustainable sourcing, and circular economy practices. By integrating these goals into its operations, IKEA ensures that its activities create value for customers and the environment.

IKEA's focus on operational alignment is also evident in its supply chain practices. The company works closely with suppliers to ensure ethical labor practices and environmental sustainability. This alignment enhances IKEA's reputation and drives customer loyalty, contributing to its long-term success.

Leveraging Technology for Strategic Alignment

Technology plays a crucial role in enhancing strategic alignment. Digital tools and platforms can facilitate communication, collaboration, and performance measurement, helping organizations stay focused on their purpose and strategic goals.

One effective approach is using data analytics to track performance and identify areas for improvement. By gathering and analyzing data on KPIs, organizations can ensure that their activities align with their strategic objectives. This data-driven approach enhances decision-making and accountability, supporting continuous improvement.

Technology can also facilitate communication and collaboration across the organization. Digital platforms can provide employees with access to resources, training, and feedback, helping them stay connected to the organization's purpose and goals. Virtual meetings, webinars, and collaboration tools can enhance coordination and engagement, fostering a culture of alignment.

Case Study: Microsoft

Microsoft leverages technology to enhance strategic alignment. The company's mission "to empower every person and every organization on the planet to achieve more" guides its efforts to create a supportive and inclusive work environment (Microsoft, n.d.).

The company's internal platforms, such as Yammer and Teams, facilitate communication and collaboration among employees, helping them stay connected to its mission. The company also offers extensive learning and development resources through its LinkedIn Learning platform, enabling employees to grow their skills and align their careers with Microsoft's purpose.

Microsoft's use of technology extends to its performance management system, which includes regular check-ins, feedback, and recognition. This approach ensures that employees receive the support and guidance they need to succeed and stay engaged. By leveraging technology to foster strategic alignment, Microsoft has built a motivated and high-performing workforce.

The company's focus on leveraging technology for alignment is further reflected in its data-driven decision-making processes. Microsoft uses advanced analytics to track progress toward its strategic goals and identify areas for improvement. This approach enhances transparency and accountability, ensuring that Microsoft's strategy remains aligned with its purpose.

The Role of Leadership in Strategic Alignment

Leadership is critical for achieving and maintaining strategic alignment. Leaders should articulate a clear vision that aligns with the organization's purpose and inspire employees to contribute their best efforts. They should also provide the resources, support, and autonomy needed for alignment to flourish.

Effective leaders model aligned behaviors, demonstrating a commitment to the organization's purpose in their actions and decisions. They communicate the organization's purpose consistently, ensuring that employees understand and embrace its mission. Leaders also create an environment where alignment is valued and rewarded, enhancing engagement and performance.

Leaders play a pivotal role in ensuring that the organization's strategy remains aligned with its purpose. This role involves regularly reviewing and adjusting the strategy based on feedback and changing circumstances. Leaders must be adaptable and open to new ideas, ensuring that the organization remains focused on its long-term goals.

Case Study: Apple under Tim Cook

Tim Cook's leadership at Apple exemplifies the importance of strategic alignment. Apple's purpose "to create the best products on earth and to leave the world better than we found it" guides Cook's vision and decision-making (Apple, n.d.). He emphasizes innovation, quality, and sustainability, aligning Apple's strategy with its purpose.

Cook fosters a culture of alignment by integrating Apple's purpose into all aspects of its operations. He emphasizes the importance of design excellence, customer experience, and environmental responsibility. Under his leadership, Apple has developed iconic products such as the iPhone, iPad, and MacBook, which reflect the company's commitment to quality and innovation.

Tim Cook's leadership style exemplifies the importance of setting a clear vision and inspiring a culture of alignment. His focus on aligning product development with Apple's purpose has helped create groundbreaking technologies that have had a profound impact on the industry and society.

Measuring the Impact of Strategic Alignment

Measuring the impact of strategic alignment is essential for demonstrating its value and ensuring accountability. Organizations can use various metrics to assess the effectiveness of their efforts toward alignment with the organization's purpose.

KPIs for strategic alignment may include financial metrics, such as revenue growth and return on investment, as well as non-financial metrics, such as customer satisfaction, employee engagement, and sustainability. Regularly reviewing and reporting on these metrics can provide insights into the effectiveness of alignment initiatives and help identify areas for improvement.

Organizations can use performance management systems, balanced scorecards, and impact assessments to track and communicate the performance of their alignment efforts. Transparency in reporting helps build trust with stakeholders and demonstrates the organization's commitment to strategic alignment.

Case Study: Novo Nordisk

Novo Nordisk, a global healthcare company, measures the impact of its strategic alignment using its "Triple Bottom Line" approach, which evaluates performance based on financial, social, and environmental criteria. The company's purpose "to drive change to defeat diabetes and other serious chronic diseases" guides its alignment efforts and impact assessment (Novo Nordisk, n.d.).

The company's KPIs include measures of patient outcomes, access to healthcare, and environmental sustainability. By regularly reviewing and reporting on these metrics, the company demonstrates the value of its strategic alignment and ensures accountability. This holistic approach has enhanced Novo Nordisk's reputation and driven its success in the healthcare industry.

Novo Nordisk's comprehensive approach to measuring the impact of its alignment efforts highlights the importance of using a balanced set of metrics that reflect the organization's purpose and long-term goals. This transparency and accountability help build trust with stakeholders and drive continuous improvement.

Sustaining Strategic Alignment

Sustaining strategic alignment requires ongoing commitment and effort from leaders. This process involves continuously reinforcing the organization's purpose, providing support and resources, and adapting to changing circumstances while staying true to the organization's values.

Leaders should regularly revisit and reaffirm the organization's purpose, ensuring that it remains relevant and inspiring. They should also recognize and reward employees who demonstrate alignment with the organization's mission, reinforcing the importance of purpose-driven behavior.

Sustaining alignment involves creating a culture of continuous improvement, where employees are encouraged to provide feedback and contribute to the organization's success. Leaders should be open to new ideas and be willing to adapt their strategies to better align with the organization's purpose and goals.

Case Study: The Body Shop

The Body Shop's commitment to strategic alignment is reflected in its mission "to fight for a fairer and more beautiful world" (The Body Shop, n.d.). The company's leaders prioritize creating a work environment that aligns with this mission and fosters strategic alignment.

The company sustains alignment by involving employees in its social and environmental initiatives. The Body Shop encourages employees to participate in activism and volunteer activities, providing paid time off for these efforts. This alignment with the company's purpose enhances employee satisfaction and motivation.

The Body Shop's focus on transparency and open communication further supports strategic alignment. The company regularly shares updates on its social and environmental impact, ensuring that employees feel informed and connected to the organization's mission. By sustaining strategic alignment, The Body Shop has built a motivated and committed workforce that drives its long-term success.

The company's commitment to sustainability and social responsibility is also reflected in its product development and sourcing practices. The Body Shop prioritizes cruelty-free and sustainable ingredients, working closely with suppliers to ensure ethical standards are met. This alignment enhances its brand reputation and customer loyalty.

Conclusion

Strategic alignment is essential for ensuring that an organization's activities and goals are in harmony with its overarching purpose. By aligning purpose with strategy, leaders can create a unified direction that guides decision-making, resource allocation, and performance measurement. Through real-world examples and practical strategies, this chapter has highlighted the critical role of strategic alignment in transforming organizations and creating lasting value. By fostering a culture of alignment, leveraging technology, and measuring impact, leaders can ensure that their organizations thrive and contribute positively to society.

References

Apple. (n.d.). About Apple. https://www.apple.com/about/

Kaplan, R. S., & Norton, D. P. (1996). The balanced scorecard: Translating strategy into action. Harvard Business School Press.

Henderson, J. C., & Venkatraman, N. (1993). Strategic alignment: Leveraging information technology for transforming organizations. IBM Systems Journal, 32(1), 4-16.

IKEA. (n.d.). People & Planet Positive. https://www.ikea.com/ms/en_JP/about_ikea/people_and_planet/

Microsoft. (n.d.). About Microsoft. https://www.microsoft.com/en-us/about

Novo Nordisk. (n.d.). About us. https://www.novonordisk.com/about.html

Patagonia. (n.d.). Mission Statement. https://www.patagonia.com/mission-statement/

The Body Shop. (n.d.). Our Commitment. https://www.thebodyshop.com/en-us/about-us/a/a00005

Unilever. (n.d.). Sustainable Living. https://www.unilever.com/sustainable-living/

Zappos. (n.d.). Core Values. https://www.zappos.com/about/core-values

CHAPTER 4

Purpose-Driven Employee Engagement

Introduction

Employee engagement is crucial for organizational success, influencing productivity, retention, innovation, and overall performance. Although various factors contribute to engagement, a clear and compelling organizational purpose can be a powerful motivator, aligning employees' efforts with the organization's mission and values. This chapter explores the concept of purpose-driven employee engagement, detailing how an organization can leverage its purpose to foster a motivated, committed, and high-performing workforce. By examining theoretical frameworks, practical strategies, and real-world examples, we will understand how aligning purpose with employee engagement can transform organizations and create lasting value.

The Importance of Employee Engagement

Employee engagement refers to the emotional and intellectual commitment of employees to their organization. Engaged employees are motivated to contribute to the organization's success, feel a sense of ownership and pride in their work, and are willing to surpass their job expectations. High levels of engagement are associated with numerous benefits, including increased productivity, reduced turnover, improved customer satisfaction, and enhanced innovation.

Organizations with engaged employees enjoy a competitive advantage, as their workforce is more agile, resilient, and capable of delivering exceptional performance. Engaged employees are also more likely to act as brand ambassadors, portraying the organization positively to external stakeholders.

Employee engagement impacts various aspects of organizational performance, from operational efficiency to financial results. Engaged employees are more likely to collaborate, innovate, and contribute to a positive workplace culture. Conversely, disengaged employees have higher absenteeism, lower productivity, and increased turnover, which can be costly and disruptive for organizations.

The Role of Purpose in Employee Engagement

A clear and compelling purpose provides employees with a sense of meaning and direction in their work. When employees understand how their efforts contribute to a larger mission, they are more likely to feel motivated, committed, and engaged. Purpose-driven engagement involves aligning employees' personal values with the organization's purpose, creating a sense of shared goals and mutual benefit.

Purpose acts as a guiding star, helping employees navigate challenges and stay focused on the bigger picture. It fosters a sense of belonging and community, as employees feel connected to something larger than themselves. Purpose-driven organizations create environments where employees are inspired to bring their best selves to work and contribute to meaningful outcomes.

Organizations that articulate and communicate their purpose effectively can foster a deeper connection with the employees. This connection can enhance job satisfaction, loyalty, and overall engagement, driving long-term success.

Theoretical Frameworks for Purpose-Driven Employee Engagement

Several theoretical frameworks provide insights into how purpose can drive employee engagement. One such framework is the Self-Determination

Theory, which holds that individuals are motivated by the need for autonomy, competence, and relatedness (Deci & Ryan, 2000). When employees' work aligns with their values and provides opportunities for growth and connection, they are more likely to be engaged and motivated.

Another relevant framework is the Job Characteristics Model, which suggests that certain job characteristics—such as task significance, autonomy, and feedback—enhance employee motivation and satisfaction (Hackman & Oldham, 1976). Purpose-driven organizations can design roles and responsibilities that align with these characteristics, fostering higher levels of engagement.

Purpose-driven engagement also aligns with the concept of "Meaningful Work," which emphasizes the importance of finding purpose and significance in one's job. Research indicates that employees who perceive their work as meaningful are more likely to be engaged, perform better, and experience higher well-being (Rosso, Dekas, & Wrzesniewski, 2010).

Case Study: Google

Google's mission "to organize the world's information and make it universally accessible and useful" exemplifies purpose-driven employee engagement (Google, n.d.). This purpose guides Google's efforts to create a positive work environment, foster innovation, and engage employees in meaningful work.

The company's commitment to purpose-driven engagement is reflected in its initiatives, such as "20% time," where employees can spend 20% of their work hours on projects they are passionate about. This autonomy and alignment with the company's mission foster high levels of engagement and innovation. By providing opportunities for employees to work on meaningful projects that align with the organization's purpose, Google has built a motivated and committed workforce.

Google's focus on creating a supportive and inclusive culture further enhances employee engagement. The company offers extensive resources for professional development, wellness programs, and opportunities for collaboration. These initiatives align with Google's mission and create an environment where employees feel valued and engaged.

Strategies for Fostering Purpose-Driven Engagement

Creating purpose-driven engagement requires intentional strategies that align employees' roles, responsibilities, and experiences with the organization's purpose. Leaders play a crucial role in articulating the organization's purpose, communicating it consistently, and embedding it into the organizational culture.

One effective strategy is involving employees in defining and refining the organization's purpose. This participatory approach ensures that the purpose resonates with employees and reflects their values and aspirations. Leaders can organize workshops, focus groups, and surveys to gather input and build a shared understanding of the organization's mission.

Another strategy is aligning performance management systems with the organization's purpose. This approach involves setting clear expectations, providing regular feedback, and recognizing and rewarding behaviors aligned with the organization's values. Purpose-driven performance management reinforces the importance of the organization's mission and motivates employees to contribute to its success.

Organizations can also create purpose-driven development programs that provide employees with opportunities to grow and align their careers with the organization's mission. Examples include mentorship programs, leadership development initiatives, and career paths that highlight how employees' contributions support the organization's purpose.

Case Study: Salesforce

Salesforce's purpose is "to empower companies to connect with their customers in a whole new way" and guide its employee engagement efforts (Salesforce, n.d.). The company's leaders prioritize creating a positive and inclusive work environment that aligns with this purpose.

The company's "Ohana" culture, which means family in Hawaiian, emphasizes trust, customer success, innovation, and equality. This cultural framework guides the company's engagement initiatives, including its extensive employee resource groups, volunteer opportunities, and continuous learning programs. By aligning its engagement efforts with its purpose, Salesforce has built a highly motivated and committed workforce.

Salesforce's commitment to purpose-driven engagement is also reflected in its corporate social responsibility (CSR) initiatives. The company encourages employees to participate in volunteer activities and offers paid volunteer time off. This alignment with the company's purpose enhances employee satisfaction and engagement, as employees feel they are making a positive impact both inside and outside the workplace.

Leveraging Technology for Employee Engagement

Technology plays a crucial role in enhancing purpose-driven employee engagement. Digital tools and platforms can facilitate communication, collaboration, and recognition, helping employees stay connected to the organization's purpose and each other.

Employee engagement platforms can provide personalized experiences, offering resources for professional development, wellness programs, and opportunities for feedback and recognition. These platforms can also help leaders communicate the organization's purpose consistently, ensuring that employees understand how their work contributes to the larger mission.

Social media and collaboration tools can foster a sense of community and belonging, enabling employees to connect and collaborate regardless of location. Virtual events, town halls, and webinars can provide opportunities for employees to engage with leadership and stay informed about the organization's goals and initiatives.

Case Study: Microsoft

Microsoft leverages technology to enhance purpose-driven employee engagement. The company's mission "to empower every person and every organization on the planet to achieve more" guides its efforts to create a supportive and inclusive work environment (Microsoft, n.d.).

The company's internal platforms, such as Yammer and Teams, facilitate communication and collaboration among employees, helping them stay connected to the company's mission. Microsoft also offers extensive learning and development resources through its LinkedIn Learning platform, enabling employees to grow their skills and align their careers with Microsoft's purpose.

Microsoft's use of technology extends to its performance management system, which includes regular check-ins, feedback, and recognition. This approach ensures that employees receive the support and guidance they need to succeed and stay engaged. By leveraging technology to foster purpose-driven engagement, Microsoft has built a motivated and high-performing workforce.

The company's focus on creating an inclusive and supportive work environment is further reflected in its diversity and inclusion initiatives. Microsoft uses technology to track and measure progress in these areas, ensuring that its purpose-driven engagement efforts are effective and impactful.

The Impact of Purpose-Driven Engagement on Performance

Purpose-driven employee engagement has a significant impact on organizational performance. Research indicates that engaged employees are more productive, innovative, and committed to their organization's success. They are also more likely to stay with the organization, reducing turnover and associated costs.

Engaged employees are motivated to surpass their job expectations, contributing to higher levels of customer satisfaction and loyalty. They are also more likely to collaborate and share ideas, driving innovation and continuous improvement. Purpose-driven engagement fosters a positive work environment, enhancing overall organizational performance.

Organizations with high levels of employee engagement also tend to have stronger financial performance. Engaged employees are more efficient and effective, leading to increased profitability and growth. Purpose-driven engagement also enhances the organization's reputation, attracting top talent and building customer trust.

Case Study: Southwest Airlines

Southwest Airlines' purpose "to connect people to what's important in their lives through friendly, reliable, and low-cost air travel" drives its employee engagement efforts (Southwest Airlines, n.d.). The company's leaders prioritize creating a positive and supportive work environment that aligns with this purpose.

Southwest's "Servant's Heart" culture emphasizes teamwork, respect, and customer service. This cultural framework guides the company's engagement initiatives, including its extensive employee recognition programs, professional development opportunities, and community involvement. By aligning its engagement efforts with its purpose, Southwest has built a highly motivated and committed workforce.

The airline's commitment to purpose-driven engagement is reflected in its performance. Southwest consistently ranks high in customer satisfaction and employee engagement surveys. Its focus on creating a positive work environment and aligning employee efforts with its purpose has contributed to its long-term success and profitability.

Southwest's approach to employee engagement also includes regular communication and feedback. The company holds town hall meetings and surveys to gather employee input and ensure alignment with its purpose. This transparency and inclusivity help build trust and commitment among employees.

Sustaining Purpose-Driven Engagement

Sustaining purpose-driven employee engagement requires ongoing commitment and effort from leaders. This approach involves continuously reinforcing the organization's purpose, providing support and resources, and adapting to changing circumstances while staying true to the organization's values.

Leaders should regularly revisit and reaffirm the organization's purpose, ensuring that it remains relevant and inspiring. They should also recognize and reward employees who demonstrate engagement and alignment with the organization's mission, reinforcing the importance of purpose-driven behavior.

Sustaining engagement involves creating a culture of continuous improvement, where employees are encouraged to provide feedback and contribute to the organization's success. Leaders should be open to new ideas and be willing to adapt their strategies to better align with the organization's purpose and goals.

Case Study: Patagonia

Patagonia's commitment to purpose-driven employee engagement is reflected in its mission "to build the best product, cause no unnecessary harm, use business to inspire and implement solutions to the environmental crisis" (Patagonia, n.d.). The company's leaders prioritize creating a work environment that aligns with this mission and fosters employee engagement.

The company sustains engagement by involving employees in its environmental and social initiatives. Patagonia encourages employees to participate in activism and volunteer activities, providing paid time off for these efforts. This alignment with the company's purpose enhances employee satisfaction and motivation.

Patagonia's focus on transparency and open communication further supports purpose-driven engagement. The company regularly shares updates on its environmental impact and social initiatives, ensuring that employees feel informed and connected to the organization's mission. By sustaining purpose-driven engagement, Patagonia has built a motivated and committed workforce that drives its long-term success.

Patagonia's commitment to sustainability and social responsibility is also reflected in its supply chain practices. The company works closely with suppliers to ensure ethical and sustainable practices, reinforcing its purpose and enhancing employee engagement.

Measuring the Impact of Purpose-Driven Engagement

Measuring the impact of purpose-driven engagement is essential for demonstrating value and ensuring accountability. Organizations can use various metrics to assess the effectiveness of their engagement efforts and their alignment with the organization's purpose.

KPIs for purpose-driven engagement may include employee satisfaction, retention rates, productivity, and performance metrics. Regularly reviewing and reporting on these metrics can provide insights into the effectiveness of engagement initiatives and identify areas for improvement.

Organizations can use employee surveys, feedback tools, and performance management systems to gather data on engagement levels and identify trends. Transparent reporting helps build trust with employees and demonstrates the organization's commitment to purpose-driven engagement.

Case Study: Novo Nordisk

Novo Nordisk, a global healthcare company, measures the impact of its purpose-driven engagement through its "Triple Bottom Line" approach, which evaluates performance based on financial, social, and environmental criteria. The company's purpose "to drive change to defeat diabetes and other serious chronic diseases" guides its engagement efforts and impact assessment (Novo Nordisk, n.d.).

Novo Nordisk's KPIs include measures of employee satisfaction, retention, and productivity, as well as patient outcomes and environmental sustainability. By regularly reviewing and reporting on these metrics, the company demonstrates the value of its purpose-driven engagement and ensures accountability. This holistic approach has enhanced Novo Nordisk's reputation and driven its success in the healthcare industry.

The company's comprehensive approach to measuring the impact of its engagement efforts highlights the importance of using a balanced set of metrics that reflect the organization's purpose and long-term goals. Transparency and accountability help build trust with employees and drive continuous improvement.

Conclusion

Purpose-driven employee engagement is a powerful strategy for creating a motivated, committed, and high-performing workforce. By aligning employees' roles, responsibilities, and experiences with the organization's purpose, leaders can foster a sense of meaning and direction that enhances engagement and drives long-term success. Through real-world examples and practical strategies, this chapter has highlighted the critical role of purpose-driven engagement in transforming organizations and creating lasting value. By sustaining engagement efforts and measuring their impact, leaders can ensure that their organizations thrive and contribute positively to society.

References

Deci, E. L., & Ryan, R. M. (2000). The "what" and "why" of goal pursuits: Human needs and the self-determination of behavior. Psychological Inquiry, 11(4), 227-268.

Google. (n.d.). About Google. https://about.google/

Hackman, J. R., & Oldham, G. R. (1976). Motivation through the design of work: Test of a theory. Organizational Behavior and Human Performance, 16(2), 250-279.

Microsoft. (n.d.). About Microsoft. https://www.microsoft.com/en-us/about

Novo Nordisk. (n.d.). About us. https://www.novonordisk.com/about.html

Patagonia. (n.d.). Mission Statement. https://www.patagonia.com/mission-statement/

Rosso, B. D., Dekas, K. H., & Wrzesniewski, A. (2010). On the meaning of work: A theoretical integration and review. Research in Organizational Behavior, 30, 91-127.

Salesforce. (n.d.). Our story. https://www.salesforce.com/company/

Southwest Airlines. (n.d.). About Southwest Airlines. https://www.southwest.com/html/about-southwest/

CHAPTER 5

Purpose-Driven Innovation

Introduction

In today's rapidly evolving business landscape, innovation is a critical driver of competitive advantage and long-term success. However, innovation that is guided by a higher purpose can transcend traditional boundaries, creating value that benefits not only the organization but also society. This chapter explores the concept of purpose-driven innovation, detailing how organizations can leverage their purpose to inspire creativity, drive growth, and make a positive impact on the world. By examining theoretical frameworks, practical strategies, and real-world examples, we will understand how purpose-driven innovation can transform organizations and create lasting value.

The Relationship Between Purpose and Innovation

Innovation involves the creation and implementation of new ideas, products, processes, or services that deliver value. Although innovation can occur in any organization, purpose-driven innovation is characterized by its alignment with the organization's higher purpose and values. This alignment ensures that innovation efforts are not only focused on financial success but also on achieving broader societal, environmental, and ethical goals.

Purpose provides a clear direction and motivation for innovation. Organizational purpose inspires employees to think creatively and take risks, knowing that their efforts will contribute to a meaningful cause.

When innovation is driven by purpose, it can lead to more sustainable and impactful solutions, fostering a culture of continuous improvement and social responsibility.

Organizations with a clear purpose can harness their mission to guide their innovation strategies, ensuring that new developments align with their core values and long-term objectives. This alignment helps create innovations that resonate with stakeholders and address pressing societal issues, enhancing the organization's overall impact.

Theoretical Frameworks for Purpose-Driven Innovation

Several theoretical frameworks provide insights into how purpose can drive innovation. One such framework is the "Jobs to be Done" theory, which suggests that customers "hire" products or services to achieve specific outcomes or solve problems (Christensen, 2016). By understanding the underlying needs and motivations of customers, organizations can develop innovative solutions aligned with their purpose and create significant value.

Another relevant framework is the concept of "disruptive innovation," introduced by Clayton Christensen. Disruptive innovation involves creating products or services that initially serve a niche market but eventually transform the industry by offering more accessible and affordable solutions (Christensen, 1997). Purpose-driven organizations can leverage disruptive innovation to address societal challenges and create positive change.

Purpose-driven innovation also ties into the "Triple Bottom Line" framework, which emphasizes balancing economic, social, and environmental outcomes. This approach ensures that innovation efforts contribute to financial performance while also addressing social equity and environmental sustainability, aligning with the organization's overarching purpose.

Case Study: Tesla

Tesla's mission "to accelerate the world's transition to sustainable energy" exemplifies purpose-driven innovation (Tesla, n.d.). This purpose guides Tesla's innovation efforts, resulting in groundbreaking products such as electric vehicles (EVs), solar energy solutions, and energy storage systems.

The company's focus on sustainability has driven its research and development initiatives, leading to significant advancements in battery technology, autonomous driving, and renewable energy. By aligning its innovation efforts with its purpose, Tesla has not only disrupted the automotive industry but also contributed to global efforts to combat climate change.

Tesla's innovative approach extends beyond product development to its business model, including direct-to-consumer sales and the creation of a robust charging infrastructure. These innovations, which are aligned with its purpose, have helped Tesla build a loyal customer base and set new standards for the automotive and energy industries.

Fostering a Culture of Innovation

Creating a culture that supports purpose-driven innovation requires intentional effort from leaders. This approach involves fostering an environment where creativity and experimentation are encouraged, and employees feel empowered to take risks and share ideas. Leaders should model innovative behaviors, provide resources and support, and recognize and reward innovative efforts.

One effective strategy for fostering a culture of innovation is to establish innovation labs or centers of excellence. These dedicated spaces allow employees to collaborate on new ideas, test prototypes, and develop innovative solutions. Innovation labs can also serve as incubators for new business ventures, providing a structured environment for exploring and scaling purpose-driven innovations.

Organizations can also implement processes and practices that encourage innovation, such as design thinking workshops, hackathons, and cross-functional teams. Providing employees with time and resources to work on passion projects can further stimulate creative thinking and align innovation efforts with the organization's purpose.

Case Study: Google X

Google X, the innovation lab of Alphabet Inc., is designed to foster a culture of purpose-driven innovation. The company's mission is to "solve big problems and build radical new technologies to make the world a better place" (Google X, n.d.). The lab operates under the principle of "moonshot thinking," encouraging employees to pursue ambitious projects that have the potential to create transformative change.

Projects developed at Google X include self-driving cars, delivery drones, and internet balloons. These initiatives align with Google's broader purpose of organizing the world's information and making it universally accessible and useful. By creating a dedicated space for innovation and aligning its efforts with its purpose, Google X has generated groundbreaking solutions that address global challenges.

Google X's focus on moonshot projects demonstrates the value of setting ambitious goals that align with organizational purpose. This approach encourages employees to think beyond incremental improvements and strive for breakthroughs that can have a significant impact on society.

Aligning Innovation with Sustainable Development Goals

The United Nations Sustainable Development Goals (SDGs) provide a global framework for addressing pressing societal and environmental challenges. Purpose-driven organizations can align their innovation efforts with the SDGs, contributing to global sustainability and social progress.

By integrating the SDGs into their innovation strategies, organizations can identify opportunities to create value that extends beyond financial returns. This alignment ensures that innovation efforts support broader goals such as poverty reduction, health and well-being, clean energy, and climate action.

Aligning innovation with the SDGs involves setting specific, measurable goals related to sustainability and social impact, incorporating these goals into the organization's strategic planning, and regularly reporting on progress. This approach helps organizations stay focused on creating positive change and achieve business success.

Case Study: Unilever

Unilever's Sustainable Living Plan demonstrates how purpose-driven innovation can align with the SDGs. The plan focuses on improving health and well-being, reducing environmental impact, and enhancing livelihoods. Unilever's innovation efforts are guided by its purpose of making sustainable living commonplace (Unilever, n.d.).

The company has developed numerous innovative products and initiatives that align with the SDGs. For example, Unilever's "Lifebuoy" soap brand promotes hand washing to prevent disease, contributing to SDG 3 (Good Health and Well-being). Unilever's commitment to sustainable sourcing and reducing plastic waste aligns with SDG 12 (Responsible Consumption and Production) and SDG 14 (Life Below Water). By integrating the SDGs into its innovation strategy, Unilever has created products that deliver social and environmental benefits while driving business growth.

Unilever's approach demonstrates the potential for purpose-driven innovation to address complex global challenges. By aligning its innovation efforts with the SDGs, Unilever has positioned itself as a leader in sustainable business practices and created a significant positive impact.

Leveraging Technology for Purpose-Driven Innovation

Technology plays a critical role in enabling purpose-driven innovation. Advances in digital technologies, such as artificial intelligence (AI), blockchain, and the Internet of Things (IoT), provide new opportunities for organizations to develop innovative solutions that address complex challenges.

Leaders should stay informed about emerging technologies and explore how they can be applied to achieve the organization's purpose. This approach requires investing in research and development, collaborating with technology partners, and fostering a culture of digital literacy and experimentation.

For instance, AI can be used to develop personalized health solutions, optimize energy usage, or improve supply chain transparency. Blockchain can enhance traceability and trust in ethical sourcing, whereas IoT can lead to smart, connected solutions that improve quality of life and reduce environmental impact.

Case Study: IBM

IBM's commitment to purpose-driven innovation is reflected in its focus on using technology to create a smarter and more sustainable world. IBM's purpose is to "be essential to our clients, to the world, and to each other" (IBM, n.d.). This purpose guides the company's innovation efforts, resulting in groundbreaking solutions that leverage advanced technologies.

One example is IBM's "Watson" AI platform, which has been used to develop solutions in healthcare, environmental management, and disaster response. IBM's "Blockchain for Good" initiative leverages blockchain technology to enhance transparency and accountability in supply chains by supporting ethical sourcing and reducing fraud. By aligning its technological innovations with its purpose, IBM has created solutions that deliver significant social and environmental benefits.

IBM's use of AI and blockchain illustrates how advanced technologies can be harnessed to drive purpose-driven innovation. By focusing on applications that align with its purpose, IBM has developed solutions that address critical societal challenges and create long-term value.

Collaborating for Innovation

Collaboration is essential for driving purpose-driven innovation. By collaborating with other organizations, research institutions, and stakeholders, companies can leverage diverse perspectives, share resources, and accelerate the development of innovative solutions.

Open innovation, which involves collaborating with external partners to co-create and share knowledge, can enhance an organization's innovation capabilities. This approach fosters a culture of collaboration and inclusivity, enabling organizations to tap into a broader pool of ideas and expertise.

Collaborative innovation can take many forms, including joint ventures, research partnerships, and innovation networks. By working together, organizations can address complex challenges more effectively and create solutions that have a greater impact.

Case Study: The Ellen MacArthur Foundation and the Circular Economy

The Ellen MacArthur Foundation (EMF) is dedicated to promoting the transition to a circular economy, where products and materials are reused, remanufactured, and recycled to minimize waste. EMF collaborates with businesses, governments, and academia to drive purpose-driven innovation and systemic change (Ellen MacArthur Foundation, n.d.).

Through its collaboration with companies such as Philips, Google, and Unilever, EMF has developed innovative solutions that align with the principles of the circular economy. These initiatives include designing products for longevity, creating closed-loop supply chains, and developing business models that prioritize resource efficiency. By fostering collaboration and aligning innovation efforts with its purpose, EMF has accelerated the adoption of circular economy practices and driven positive environmental impact.

EMF's collaborative approach highlights the importance of partnerships in achieving purpose-driven innovation. By working together, organizations can leverage their collective expertise and resources to drive systemic change and create a more sustainable future.

Building Resilient and Adaptable Organizations

Purpose-driven innovation requires organizations to be resilient and adaptable in the face of change. Leaders should create an environment where continuous learning and adaptation are valued, and employees are empowered to respond to new challenges and opportunities.

This approach involves fostering a growth mindset, encouraging experimentation, and providing support for professional development. By creating a culture of resilience and adaptability, organizations can navigate uncertainty and drive sustained innovation.

Building resilience can be achieved by implementing agile methodologies, investing in employee development, and creating processes that allow rapid iteration and feedback. These practices help organizations remain flexible and responsive to changing market conditions and emerging opportunities.

Case Study: 3M

3M's commitment to innovation and adaptability has enabled it to thrive for over a century. The company's purpose is "to improve every life through innovative giving in education, community, and the environment" (3M, n.d.). This purpose guides 3M's innovation efforts and supports its culture of continuous improvement.

The company's "15% rule" encourages employees to spend 15% of their time on projects of their choosing, fostering creativity and experimentation. The company's collaborative research and development processes, known as "Tech Forums," enable employees to share knowledge and develop cross-disciplinary solutions. By promoting a culture of resilience and adaptability, 3M has consistently delivered innovative products that are aligned with its purpose and address global challenges.

3M's approach to fostering innovation highlights the importance of providing employees with the freedom and support to explore new ideas. This culture of continuous improvement and adaptability has enabled 3M to maintain its competitive edge and drive purpose-driven innovation.

The Role of Leadership in Purpose-Driven Innovation

Leadership is critical for driving purpose-driven innovation. Leaders should articulate a clear vision that aligns with the organization's purpose and inspire employees to contribute their best efforts. Providing the resources, support, and autonomy needed for innovation to flourish is also important.

Leaders should model innovative behaviors, embrace failure as a learning opportunity, and recognize and reward innovative contributions. By creating an environment that supports purpose-driven innovation, leaders can harness the creativity and passion of their employees to achieve the organization's goals.

Effective leadership involves setting a clear innovation strategy, fostering a culture of trust and collaboration, and removing barriers that impede creativity. Leaders play a pivotal role in ensuring that the organization's innovation efforts align with its purpose and create meaningful impact.

Case Study: Apple under Steve Jobs

Steve Jobs' leadership at Apple is a quintessential example of purpose-driven innovation. Apple's purpose "to create the best products on earth and to leave the world better than we found it" guided Jobs' vision and decision-making (Apple, n.d.). He emphasized design excellence, user experience, and seamless integration of hardware and software.

Jobs fostered a culture of innovation by encouraging employees to "think different" and pursue bold ideas. Under his leadership, Apple developed iconic products such as the iPhone, iPad, and MacBook, which revolutionized the technology industry and transformed how people interact with technology. By aligning innovation efforts with Apple's purpose, Jobs created products that delivered exceptional value and made a lasting impact on the world.

Steve Jobs' leadership style exemplified the importance of setting a clear vision and inspiring a culture of innovation. His focus on aligning product development with Apple's purpose helped create groundbreaking technologies that have had a profound impact on the industry and society.

Embedding Purpose-Driven Innovation into Strategy

Integrating purpose-driven innovation into the organization's strategic planning ensures that innovation efforts support the organization's long-term goals. This approach involves aligning innovation initiatives with the organization's mission, values, and objectives.

Leaders should develop a strategic roadmap that outlines key innovation priorities, milestones, and metrics. This roadmap should be communicated clearly to all stakeholders to ensure alignment and accountability. Regularly reviewing and adjusting the strategy based on feedback and changing circumstances can enhance the organization's ability to achieve its innovation goals.

Embedding purpose-driven innovation into strategy requires a comprehensive approach that includes setting clear innovation goals, allocating resources, and establishing governance structures that support innovation. This alignment ensures that innovation efforts are consistent with the organization's purpose and drive sustainable success.

Case Study: Danone

Danone's purpose "to bring health through food to as many people as possible" is embedded into its strategic planning and innovation efforts (Danone, n.d.). The company's "One Planet. One Health" framework guides its commitment to sustainable development and health-focused innovation.

The company's strategic initiatives include developing healthier products, reducing environmental impact, and supporting sustainable agriculture. Danone's innovation efforts, such as plant-based products and regenerative farming practices, align with its purpose and address global health and environmental challenges. By embedding purpose-driven innovation into its strategy, Danone has created a positive impact on society and strengthened its market position.

Danone's integrated approach to innovation and sustainability demonstrates the importance of aligning strategic planning with organizational purpose. This alignment has enabled Danone to develop innovative solutions that contribute to its mission and drive long-term success.

Overcoming Barriers to Purpose-Driven Innovation

Despite the benefits of purpose-driven innovation, organizations certain barriers may hinder organizations' efforts. Common challenges include resistance to change, limited resources, and misalignment between purpose and business goals. Leaders should proactively address these barriers to create an environment where purpose-driven innovation can thrive.

Strategies for overcoming barriers include fostering a culture of openness and inclusivity, providing resources and support for innovation, and ensuring alignment between purpose and strategic objectives. Leaders should also communicate the value of purpose-driven innovation to all stakeholders, building buy-in and support.

Addressing barriers to innovation involves creating a supportive environment where employees feel empowered to take risks and explore new ideas. Employee empowerment can involve providing training and development programs, allocating resources for innovation projects, and fostering a culture of collaboration and continuous improvement.

Case Study: Interface

Interface, a global manufacturer of modular flooring, faced significant challenges in its journey toward purpose-driven innovation. The company's purpose "to lead industry to love the world" guided its mission to become a sustainable and restorative enterprise (Interface, n.d.). However, Interface encountered resistance to change and resource constraints as it pursued its sustainability goals.

To overcome these barriers, Interface's leaders fostered a culture of inclusivity and transparency, involving employees at all levels in the company's sustainability initiatives. The company also invested in research and development to develop innovative, sustainable products and processes. By addressing barriers and aligning innovation efforts with its purpose, Interface has achieved significant progress in its sustainability journey and demonstrated the power of purpose-driven innovation.

Interface's approach highlights the importance of engaging employees and stakeholders in the innovation process. By creating a culture of inclusivity and transparency, Interface has been able to overcome challenges and drive meaningful progress toward its sustainability goals.

Measuring the Impact of Purpose-Driven Innovation

Measuring the impact of purpose-driven innovation is essential for demonstrating its value and ensuring accountability. Organizations can use various metrics to assess the success of their innovation efforts and their alignment with the organization's purpose.

KPIs for purpose-driven innovation may include financial metrics, such as revenue growth and return on investment, as well as non-financial metrics, such as environmental impact, social impact, and customer satisfaction. Regularly reviewing and reporting on these metrics can provide insights into the effectiveness of innovation initiatives and help identify areas for improvement.

Organizations can use sustainability reports, impact assessments, and dashboards to track and communicate the performance of their innovation efforts. Transparent reporting helps build trust with stakeholders and demonstrates the organization's commitment to its purpose.

Case Study: Novo Nordisk

Novo Nordisk, a global healthcare company, measures the impact of its purpose-driven innovation through its "Triple Bottom Line" approach, which evaluates performance based on financial, social, and environmental criteria. The company's purpose "to drive change to defeat diabetes and other serious chronic diseases" guides its innovation efforts and impact assessment (Novo Nordisk, n.d.).

The company's KPIs include measures of patient outcomes, access to healthcare, and environmental sustainability. By regularly reviewing and reporting on these metrics, Novo Nordisk demonstrates the value of its purpose-driven innovation and ensures accountability. This holistic approach has enhanced Novo Nordisk's reputation and driven its success in the healthcare industry.

Novo Nordisk's comprehensive approach to measuring the impact of its innovation efforts highlights the importance of using a balanced set of metrics that reflect the organization's purpose and long-term goals. This transparency and accountability help build trust with stakeholders and drive continuous improvement.

Conclusion

Purpose-driven innovation is a powerful strategy for creating value that extends beyond financial returns. By aligning innovation efforts with the organization's purpose, leaders can inspire creativity, drive growth, and make a positive impact on society and the environment. Through real-world examples and practical strategies, this chapter has highlighted the critical role of purpose-driven innovation in transforming organizations and achieving long-term success. By fostering a culture of innovation, leveraging technology, collaborating with partners, and measuring impact, leaders can ensure that their organizations thrive and contribute to a better world.

References

3M. (n.d.). About 3M. https://www.3m.com/3M/en_US/company-us/

Apple. (n.d.). About Apple. https://www.apple.com/about/

Christensen, C. M. (1997). The innovator's dilemma: When new technologies cause great firms to fail. Harvard Business School Press.

Christensen, C. M. (2016). Competing against luck: The story of innovation and customer choice. HarperBusiness.

Danone. (n.d.). Our Mission. https://www.danone.com/about-danone/our-mission.html

Ellen MacArthur Foundation. (n.d.). About us. https://www.ellenmacarthurfoundation.org/about

Google X. (n.d.). About Google X. https://x.company/about/

IBM. (n.d.). Our purpose. https://www.ibm.com/ibm/us/en/

Interface. (n.d.). Mission statement. https://www.interface.com/US/en-US/sustainability/mission-statement.html

Novo Nordisk. (n.d.). About us. https://www.novonordisk.com/about.html

Tesla. (n.d.). About Tesla. https://www.tesla.com/about

Unilever. (n.d.). Sustainable Living. https://www.unilever.com/sustainable-living/

CHAPTER 6

Ethical Leadership and the Golden Rule

Introduction

Ethical leadership is the cornerstone of a thriving, purpose-driven organization. At its heart, ethical leadership involves guiding and influencing others based on ethical principles and values. One of the most universally recognized ethical principles is the Golden Rule: "Treat others as you would like to be treated." This chapter explores the role of ethical leadership and the Golden Rule in fostering a culture of alignment and trust within organizations. By examining theoretical frameworks, practical applications, and real-world examples, we will understand how ethical leadership can enhance organizational performance and employee engagement.

The Foundations of Ethical Leadership

Ethical leaders prioritize ethical behavior and decision-making, ensuring that their actions align with moral principles and the organization's values. They serve as role models, demonstrating integrity, fairness, and empathy in their interactions with others. Ethical leaders are also committed to doing the right thing, even when it is difficult or unpopular.

The concept of ethical leadership is rooted in various ethical theories, including deontological ethics, which emphasizes duties and rules, and virtue ethics, which focuses on the character and virtues of the individual. Ethical leaders are guided by a strong sense of duty and a commitment to virtuous behavior, fostering an environment of trust and respect within their organizations (Brown & Treviño, 2006).

The Golden Rule in Leadership

The Golden Rule is a timeless ethical principle that transcends cultural and religious boundaries. It advocates treating others with the same respect, kindness, and fairness that one would expect for oneself. In the context of leadership, the Golden Rule serves as a powerful guiding principle, promoting empathy, respect, and ethical behavior.

Leaders who apply the Golden Rule in their leadership practices create a positive and supportive work environment. They prioritize the well-being of their employees, making decisions after considering their impact on all stakeholders. By treating employees, customers, and partners with respect and fairness, ethical leaders build trust and loyalty, enhancing organizational cohesion and performance.

Case Study: Marriott International

Marriott International exemplifies ethical leadership and the application of the Golden Rule in its operations. The company's founder, J. Willard Marriott, emphasized the importance of treating employees well, believing that if you take care of your employees, they will take care of the customers (Marriott International, n.d.). This philosophy has guided the company's leadership practices and contributed to its success.

The company's commitment to ethical leadership is reflected in its "Spirit to Serve" program, which focuses on employee well-being, customer satisfaction, and community involvement. Marriott's leaders prioritize ethical behavior and decision-making, creating a culture of trust and respect. This ethical foundation has helped Marriott maintain high levels of employee engagement and customer loyalty, demonstrating the power of the Golden Rule in leadership.

The Role of Trust in Ethical Leadership

Trust is a fundamental element of ethical leadership. Ethical leaders build trust by consistently demonstrating integrity, transparency, and fairness in their actions and decisions. Trust fosters a positive work environment where employees feel valued and supported, leading to higher levels of engagement and performance.

Trust is built through open and honest communication, ethical decision-making, and a commitment to doing what is right. Leaders who are transparent about their intentions and actions admit mistakes, take responsibility, and earn the trust and respect of their employees. This trust is crucial for fostering a culture of alignment and collaboration.

Case Study: Patagonia

Patagonia, an outdoor clothing company, is renowned for its commitment to ethical leadership and transparency. The company's purpose is "to save our home planet," and its leaders prioritize ethical behavior and decision-making in all aspects of the business (Patagonia, n.d.). Patagonia's leaders are transparent about the company's environmental impact, openly sharing information about its supply chain and sustainability practices.

This transparency has built trust with employees, customers, and other stakeholders, enhancing Patagonia's reputation and fostering a loyal customer base. By aligning its actions with its purpose and values, Patagonia demonstrates the power of ethical leadership and trust in building a purpose-driven organization.

Empathy and Ethical Leadership

Empathy is a key component of ethical leadership. Empathetic leaders understand and consider the feelings and perspectives of others, and thus, they make decisions that reflect care and concern for others' well-being. Empathy fosters a supportive work environment where employees feel understood and valued.

Leaders can demonstrate empathy by actively listening to employees, showing compassion, and addressing their needs and concerns. Empathy also involves recognizing and respecting diverse perspectives and experiences, promoting inclusion and equity within the organization.

Case Study: Microsoft

Under the leadership of Satya Nadella, Microsoft has embraced empathy as a core value. Nadella's leadership style is characterized by a focus on empathy, inclusivity, and empowerment. He encourages employees to "seek first to understand, then to be understood," promoting a culture of empathy and respect (Microsoft, n.d.).

Nadella's empathetic leadership has transformed Microsoft's culture, fostering innovation, collaboration, and employee engagement. By prioritizing empathy and ethical behavior, Nadella has aligned Microsoft's operations with its purpose of empowering every person and organization on the planet to achieve more.

Ethical Decision-Making

Ethical decision-making is a critical aspect of ethical leadership. Leaders should navigate complex and often ambiguous situations to make decisions that align with ethical principles and the organization's values. Ethical decision-making involves considering the impact of decisions on all stakeholders and prioritizing long-term benefits over short-term gains.

Leaders can use ethical frameworks, such as utilitarianism (which focuses on the greatest good for the greatest number) and deontological ethics (which emphasizes duties and rules), to guide their decision-making processes. Additionally, involving diverse perspectives and seeking input from stakeholders can enhance the ethical quality of their decisions.

Case Study: Johnson & Johnson

Johnson & Johnson's handling of the Tylenol crisis in 1982 is a classic example of ethical decision-making in leadership. When cyanide-laced Tylenol capsules caused several deaths, Johnson & Johnson faced a significant public health and public relations crisis. Guided by the company's Credo, which emphasizes putting the needs and well-being of the people it serves first, Johnson & Johnson made the ethical decision to recall 31 million bottles of Tylenol, prioritizing customer safety over financial considerations (Johnson & Johnson, n.d.).

This decision demonstrated Johnson & Johnson's commitment to ethical leadership and responsibility. The company's transparent and ethical response restored public trust and reinforced its reputation as a values-driven organization.

Building an Ethical Culture

An ethical culture is one where ethical behavior is the norm and is reinforced through policies, practices, and leadership. Building an ethical culture involves establishing clear ethical standards, providing training and resources, and creating mechanisms for reporting and addressing unethical behavior.

Because leaders play a crucial role in shaping and maintaining an ethical culture, they must model ethical behavior, communicate the importance of ethics, and hold themselves and others accountable to high ethical standards. Additionally, leaders should create an environment where employees feel safe to voice ethical concerns and where ethical behavior is recognized and rewarded.

Case Study: IBM

IBM's commitment to ethical leadership and culture is exemplified by its long-standing values and principles. The company's "IBM Values" emphasize its dedication to every client's success, innovation that matters, and trust and personal responsibility in all relationships (IBM, n.d.). These values guide IBM's ethical standards and decision-making processes.

The company provides comprehensive ethics training for employees and has established a robust ethics reporting system. IBM's leaders regularly communicate the importance of ethical behavior and recognize employees who demonstrate integrity. By embedding ethics into its culture, IBM fosters a work environment where ethical behavior is expected and rewarded.

The Impact of Ethical Leadership on Employee Engagement

Ethical leadership has a significant impact on employee engagement. When employees perceive their leaders as ethical and trustworthy, they are more likely to feel valued, motivated, and committed to the organization. Ethical leadership creates a positive work environment where employees are encouraged to contribute their best efforts and align their actions with the organization's purpose.

Research has shown that ethical leadership is positively correlated with job satisfaction, organizational commitment, and employee performance (Brown, Treviño, & Harrison, 2005). By prioritizing ethical behavior and decision-making, leaders can enhance employee engagement and drive organizational success.

Case Study: Google

Google's commitment to ethical leadership and employee well-being has contributed to its reputation as one of the best places to work. The company's leaders prioritize transparency, fairness, and respect in their interactions with employees. Google's purpose "to organize the world's information and make it universally accessible and useful" is reflected in its ethical practices and decision-making (Google, n.d.).

The company's leaders regularly communicate with employees, seeking their input and addressing their concerns. The company's ethical leadership and supportive work environment have resulted in high levels of employee engagement and satisfaction, driving innovation and performance.

Fostering Inclusion and Equity

Ethical leadership involves promoting inclusion and equity within the organization. Leaders should ensure that all employees have equal opportunities to succeed and feel valued and respected. They can achieve this goal by addressing systemic biases, providing support and resources for underrepresented groups, and creating an inclusive culture.

Inclusive and equitable practices enhance organizational performance by fostering diverse perspectives and ideas. Leaders should prioritize diversity and inclusion in their hiring, promotion, and decision-making processes, ensuring that the organization's values are reflected in its actions.

Case Study: Salesforce

Salesforce is committed to promoting inclusion and equity through its "Equality" initiatives. The company's purpose is "to empower companies to connect with their customers in a whole new way," and this includes creating a diverse and inclusive work environment (Salesforce, n.d.). Salesforce's leadership prioritizes diversity and inclusion, implementing policies and practices that support underrepresented groups.

The company's commitment to equality includes regular assessments of pay equity, comprehensive diversity training, and support for employee resource groups. By fostering an inclusive and equitable culture, Salesforce demonstrates the importance of ethical leadership in promoting diversity and inclusion.

The Role of Corporate Social Responsibility

Corporate Social Responsibility (CSR) is an extension of ethical leadership; it involves a commitment to social and environmental stewardship. Ethical leaders recognize their responsibility to contribute positively to society and the environment, going beyond compliance to proactively address social and environmental issues.

CSR initiatives can include sustainability efforts, community engagement, and philanthropy. By integrating CSR into their operations, organizations can enhance their reputation, build trust with stakeholders, and contribute to the greater good.

Case Study: Unilever

Unilever's Sustainable Living Plan exemplifies the company's commitment to CSR and ethical leadership. The Plan's aim is to decouple Unilever's growth from its environmental footprint while increasing its positive social impact. It includes ambitious goals such as improving health and well-being, reducing environmental impact, and enhancing livelihoods (Unilever, n.d.).

The company's leaders prioritize ethical behavior and decision-making, ensuring that Unilever's actions align with its purpose of making sustainable living commonplace. This commitment to CSR has enhanced Unilever's reputation and driven its growth, demonstrating the impact of ethical leadership on organizational success.

Sustaining Ethical Leadership

Sustaining ethical leadership requires ongoing commitment and effort from leaders. This process involves continuously reinforcing ethical standards, providing support and resources, and adapting to changing circumstances while staying true to the organization's values.

Leaders should regularly revisit and reaffirm the organization's ethical principles, ensuring that they remain relevant and inspiring. They should also recognize and reward employees who demonstrate ethical behavior, reinforcing the importance of ethics. Finally, leaders should be adaptable and open to feedback, adjusting practices and policies as needed to sustain ethical leadership.

Case Study: The Body Shop

The Body Shop's commitment to ethical leadership and social responsibility has remained steadfast since it was founded. The company's purpose is "to fight for a fairer and more beautiful world," and its leaders prioritize ethical behavior and decision-making in all aspects of the business (The Body Shop, n.d.).

The company's leaders continuously reinforce its ethical principles through campaigns, partnerships, and initiatives that promote social and environmental justice. By staying true to its values and adapting to new challenges, The Body Shop has built a resilient and purpose-driven organization that supports its long-term goals.

Conclusion

Ethical leadership and the Golden Rule are fundamental to fostering a culture of alignment and trust within organizations. By prioritizing ethical behavior and decision-making, leaders can create a positive and supportive work environment that enhances organizational performance and employee engagement. Through real-world examples and practical strategies, this chapter has highlighted the critical role of ethical leadership in driving engagement, innovation, and performance. By prioritizing ethical leadership, leaders can ensure that their organizations thrive and make a positive impact on society and the environment.

References

Brown, M. E., & Treviño, L. K. (2006). Ethical leadership: A review and future directions. The Leadership Quarterly, 17(6), 595-616.

Brown, M. E., Treviño, L. K., & Harrison, D. A. (2005). Ethical leadership: A social learning perspective for construct development and testing. Organizational Behavior and Human Decision Processes, 97(2), 117-134.

Google. (n.d.). About Google. https://www.google.com/about

IBM. (n.d.). Our Values. https://www.ibm.com/ibm/history/ibm100/us/en/icons/values/

Johnson & Johnson. (n.d.). Our Credo. https://www.jnj.com/credo/

Marriott International. (n.d.). Our Story. https://www.marriott.com/marriott/aboutmarriott.mi

Microsoft. (n.d.). About Microsoft. https://www.microsoft.com/en-us/about/

Patagonia. (n.d.). Mission statement. https://www.patagonia.com/mission-statement/

Salesforce. (n.d.). Equality. https://www.salesforce.com/company/equality/

The Body Shop. (n.d.). Our Story. https://www.thebodyshop.com/about-us/our-story

Unilever. (n.d.). Sustainable Living. https://www.unilever.com/sustainable-living/

CHAPTER 7

Purpose-Driven Innovation

Introduction

In today's rapidly evolving business landscape, innovation is a critical driver of competitive advantage and long-term success. However, innovation that is guided by a higher purpose can transcend traditional boundaries, creating value that benefits not only the organization but also society. This chapter explores the concept of purpose-driven innovation, detailing how organizations can leverage their purpose to inspire creativity, drive growth, and make a positive impact on the world. By examining theoretical frameworks, practical strategies, and real-world examples, we will understand how purpose-driven innovation can transform organizations and create lasting value.

The Relationship Between Purpose and Innovation

Innovation involves the creation and implementation of new ideas, products, processes, or services that deliver value. Innovation can occur in any organization, but purpose-driven innovation is characterized by its alignment with the organization's higher purpose and values. This alignment ensures that innovation efforts are not only focused on financial success but also on achieving broader societal, environmental, and ethical goals.

Purpose provides a clear direction and motivation for innovation. It inspires employees to think creatively and take risks, knowing that their efforts contribute to a meaningful cause. Innovation that is driven by purpose can lead to more sustainable and impactful solutions, fostering a culture of continuous improvement and social responsibility.

Organizations with a clear purpose can harness their mission to guide their innovation strategies, ensuring that new developments align with their core values and long-term objectives. This alignment helps create innovations that resonate with stakeholders and address pressing societal issues, enhancing the organization's overall impact.

Theoretical Frameworks for Purpose-Driven Innovation

Several theoretical frameworks provide insights into how purpose can drive innovation. One such framework is the "Jobs to be Done" theory, which suggests that customers "hire" products or services to achieve specific outcomes or solve problems (Christensen, 2016). By understanding the underlying needs and motivations of customers, organizations can develop innovative solutions that align with their purpose and create significant value.

Another relevant framework is the concept of "disruptive innovation," introduced by Clayton Christensen. Disruptive innovation involves creating products or services that initially serve a niche market but eventually transform the industry by offering more accessible and affordable solutions (Christensen, 1997). Purpose-driven organizations can leverage disruptive innovation to address societal challenges and create positive change.

Purpose-driven innovation also ties into the "Triple Bottom Line" framework, which emphasizes balancing economic, social, and environmental outcomes. This approach ensures that innovation efforts contribute to financial performance while also addressing social equity and environmental sustainability, aligning with the organization's overarching purpose.

Case Study: Tesla

Tesla's mission "to accelerate the world's transition to sustainable energy" exemplifies purpose-driven innovation (Tesla, n.d.). This purpose guides Tesla's innovation efforts and drives the development of groundbreaking products such as electric vehicles (EVs), solar energy solutions, and energy storage systems.

The company's focus on sustainability has driven its research and development initiatives, leading to significant advancements in battery technology, autonomous driving, and renewable energy. By aligning its innovation efforts with its purpose, Tesla has not only disrupted the automotive industry but also contributed to global efforts to combat climate change.

Tesla's innovative approach extends beyond product development to its business model, including direct-to-consumer sales and the creation of a robust charging infrastructure. These innovations, aligned with its purpose, have helped Tesla build a loyal customer base and set new standards for the automotive and energy industries.

Fostering a Culture of Innovation

Creating a culture that supports purpose-driven innovation requires intentional efforts from leaders. This approach involves fostering an environment where creativity and experimentation are encouraged, and employees feel empowered to take risks and share ideas. Leaders should model innovative behaviors, provide resources and support, and recognize and reward innovative efforts.

One effective strategy for fostering a culture of innovation is to establish innovation labs or centers of excellence. These dedicated spaces allow employees to collaborate on new ideas, test prototypes, and develop innovative solutions. Innovation labs can also serve as incubators for new business ventures, providing a structured environment for exploring and scaling purpose-driven innovations.

Organizations can also implement processes and practices that encourage innovation, such as design thinking workshops, hackathons, and cross-functional teams. Providing employees with time and resources to work on passion projects can further stimulate creative thinking and align innovation efforts with the organization's purpose.

Case Study: Google X

Google X, the innovation lab of Alphabet Inc., is designed to foster a culture of purpose-driven innovation. Its mission is to "solve big problems and build radical new technologies to make the world a better place" (Google X, n.d.). The lab operates under the principle of "moonshot thinking," encouraging employees to pursue ambitious projects that have the potential to create transformative change.

Projects developed at Google X include self-driving cars, delivery drones, and internet balloons. These initiatives align with Google's broader purpose of organizing the world's information and making it universally accessible and useful. By creating a dedicated space for innovation and aligning its efforts with its purpose, Google X has generated groundbreaking solutions that address global challenges.

Google X's focus on moonshot projects demonstrates the value of setting ambitious goals that are aligned with organizational purpose. This approach encourages employees to think beyond incremental improvements and strive for breakthroughs that can have a significant impact on society.

Aligning Innovation with Sustainable Development Goals

The United Nations Sustainable Development Goals (SDGs) provide a global framework for addressing pressing societal and environmental challenges. By aligning their innovation efforts with the SDGs, purpose-driven organizations can contribute to global sustainability and social progress.

By integrating the SDGs into their innovation strategies, organizations can identify opportunities to create value that extends beyond financial returns. This alignment ensures that innovation efforts support broader goals such as poverty reduction, health and well-being, clean energy, and climate action.

Aligning innovation with the SDGs involves setting specific, measurable goals related to sustainability and social impact, incorporating these goals into the organization's strategic planning, and regularly reporting on progress. This approach helps organizations stay focused on creating positive change while achieving business success.

Case Study: Unilever

Unilever's Sustainable Living Plan demonstrates how purpose-driven innovation can align with the SDGs. The plan focuses on improving health and well-being, reducing environmental impact, and enhancing livelihoods. Unilever's innovation efforts are guided by its purpose of making sustainable living commonplace (Unilever, n.d.).

The company has developed numerous innovative products and initiatives that align with the SDGs. For example, Unilever's "Lifebuoy" soap brand promotes hand washing to prevent disease, contributing to SDG 3 (Good Health and Well-being). The company's commitment to sustainable sourcing and reducing plastic waste aligns with SDG 12 (Responsible Consumption and Production) and SDG 14 (Life Below Water). By integrating the SDGs into its innovation strategy, Unilever has created products that deliver social and environmental benefits while driving business growth.

Unilever's approach demonstrates the potential for purpose-driven innovation to address complex global challenges. By aligning its innovation efforts with the SDGs, Unilever has positioned itself as a leader in sustainable business practices and created a significant positive impact.

Leveraging Technology for Purpose-Driven Innovation

Technology plays a critical role in enabling purpose-driven innovation. Advances in digital technologies, such as artificial intelligence (AI), blockchain, and the Internet of Things (IoT), provide new opportunities for organizations to develop innovative solutions that address complex challenges.

Leaders should stay informed about emerging technologies and explore how they can be applied to achieve the organization's purpose. To achieve this goal, they must invest in research and development, collaborate with technology partners, and foster a culture of digital literacy and experimentation.

For instance, AI can be used to develop personalized health solutions, optimize energy usage, or improve supply chain transparency. Blockchain can enhance traceability and trust in ethical sourcing, whereas IoT can enable the development of smart, connected solutions that improve quality of life and reduce environmental impact.

Case Study: IBM

IBM's commitment to purpose-driven innovation is reflected in its focus on using technology to create a smarter and more sustainable world. The company's purpose is to "be essential to our clients, to the world, and to each other" (IBM, n.d.). This purpose guides the company's innovation efforts, resulting in groundbreaking solutions that leverage advanced technologies.

One example is IBM's "Watson" AI platform, which has been used to develop solutions in healthcare, environmental management, and disaster response. IBM's "Blockchain for Good" initiative leverages blockchain technology to enhance transparency and accountability in supply chains, supporting ethical sourcing and reducing fraud. By aligning its technological innovations with its purpose, IBM has created solutions that deliver significant social and environmental benefits.

IBM's use of AI and blockchain illustrates how advanced technologies can be harnessed to drive purpose-driven innovation. By focusing on applications that align with its purpose, IBM has developed solutions that address critical societal challenges and create long-term value.

Collaborating for Innovation

Collaboration is essential for driving purpose-driven innovation. By collaborating with other organizations, research institutions, and stakeholders, companies can leverage diverse perspectives, share resources, and accelerate the development of innovative solutions.

Open innovation, which involves collaborating with external partners to co-create and share knowledge, can enhance an organization's innovation capabilities. This approach fosters a culture of collaboration and inclusivity, enabling organizations to tap into a broader pool of ideas and expertise.

Collaborative innovation can take many forms, including joint ventures, research partnerships, and innovation networks. By working together, organizations can address complex challenges more effectively and create solutions that have a greater impact.

Case Study: The Ellen MacArthur Foundation and the Circular Economy

The Ellen MacArthur Foundation (EMF) is dedicated to promoting the transition to a circular economy, where products and materials are reused, remanufactured, and recycled to minimize waste. EMF collaborates with businesses, governments, and academia to drive purpose-driven innovation and systemic change (Ellen MacArthur Foundation, n.d.).

Through its collaboration with companies such as Philips, Google, and Unilever, EMF has developed innovative solutions that align with the principles of the circular economy. These initiatives include designing products for longevity, creating closed-loop supply chains, and developing business models that prioritize resource efficiency. By fostering collaboration and aligning innovation efforts with its purpose, EMF has accelerated the adoption of circular economy practices and driven positive environmental impact.

EMF's collaborative approach highlights the importance of partnerships in achieving purpose-driven innovation. By working together, organizations can leverage their collective expertise and resources to drive systemic change and create a more sustainable future.

Building Resilient and Adaptable Organizations

Purpose-driven innovation requires organizations to be resilient and adaptable in the face of change. Leaders should create an environment where continuous learning and adaptation are valued, and employees are empowered to respond to new challenges and opportunities.

This approach involves fostering a growth mindset, encouraging experimentation, and providing support for professional development. By creating a culture of resilience and adaptability, organizations can navigate uncertainty and drive sustained innovation.

Resilience can be built by implementing agile methodologies, investing in employee development, and creating processes that allow rapid iteration and feedback. These practices help organizations remain flexible and responsive to changing market conditions and emerging opportunities.

Case Study: 3M

3M's commitment to innovation and adaptability has enabled it to thrive for over a century. The company's purpose is "to improve every life through innovative giving in education, community, and the environment" (3M, n.d.). This purpose guides 3M's innovation efforts and supports its culture of continuous improvement.

3M's "15% rule" encourages employees to spend 15% of their time on projects of their choosing, fostering creativity and experimentation. The company's collaborative research and development processes, known as "Tech Forums," enable employees to share knowledge and develop cross-disciplinary solutions. By promoting a culture of resilience and adaptability, 3M has consistently delivered innovative products that align with its purpose and address global challenges.

The company's approach to fostering innovation highlights the importance of providing employees with the freedom and support to explore new ideas. This culture of continuous improvement and adaptability has enabled 3M to maintain its competitive edge and drive purpose-driven innovation.

The Role of Leadership in Purpose-Driven Innovation

Leadership is critical for driving purpose-driven innovation. Leaders should articulate a clear vision that aligns with the organization's purpose and inspire employees to contribute their best efforts. They should also provide the resources, support, and autonomy needed for innovation to flourish.

Leaders should model innovative behaviors, embrace failure as a learning opportunity, and recognize and reward innovative contributions. By creating an environment that supports purpose-driven innovation, leaders can harness the creativity and passion of their employees to achieve the organization's goals.

Effective leadership involves setting a clear innovation strategy, fostering a culture of trust and collaboration, and removing barriers that impede creativity. Leaders play a pivotal role in ensuring that the organization's innovation efforts are aligned with its purpose and create meaningful impact.

Case Study: Apple under Steve Jobs

Steve Jobs' leadership at Apple is a quintessential example of purpose-driven innovation. Apple's purpose "to create the best products on earth and to leave the world better than we found it" guided Jobs' vision and decision-making (Apple, n.d.). He emphasized design excellence, user experience, and seamless integration of hardware and software.

Jobs fostered a culture of innovation by encouraging employees to "think different" and pursue bold ideas. Under his leadership, Apple developed iconic products such as the iPhone, iPad, and MacBook, which revolutionized the technology industry and transformed how people interact with technology. By aligning innovation efforts with Apple's purpose, Jobs created products that delivered exceptional value and made a lasting impact on the world.

Steve Jobs' leadership style exemplified the importance of setting a clear vision and inspiring a culture of innovation. His focus on aligning product development with Apple's purpose helped create groundbreaking technologies that have had a profound impact on the industry and society.

Embedding Purpose-Driven Innovation into Strategy

Integrating purpose-driven innovation into the organization's strategic planning ensures that innovation efforts support the organization's long-term goals. This approach involves aligning innovation initiatives with the organization's mission, values, and objectives.

Leaders should develop a strategic roadmap that outlines key innovation priorities, milestones, and metrics. This roadmap should be communicated clearly to all stakeholders to ensure alignment and accountability. Regularly reviewing and adjusting the strategy based on feedback and changing circumstances can enhance the organization's ability to achieve its innovation goals.

Embedding purpose-driven innovation into strategy requires a comprehensive approach that includes setting clear innovation goals, allocating resources, and establishing governance structures that support innovation. This alignment ensures that innovation efforts are consistent with the organization's purpose and drive sustainable success.

Case Study: Danone

Danone's purpose "to bring health through food to as many people as possible" is embedded into its strategic planning and innovation efforts (Danone, n.d.). The company's "One Planet. One Health" framework guides its commitment to sustainable development and health-focused innovation.

The company's strategic initiatives include developing healthier products, reducing environmental impact, and supporting sustainable agriculture. Danone's innovation efforts, such as plant-based products and regenerative farming practices, align with its purpose and address global health and environmental challenges. By embedding purpose-driven innovation into its strategy, Danone has created a positive impact on society and strengthened its market position.

Danone's integrated approach to innovation and sustainability demonstrates the importance of aligning strategic planning with organizational purpose. This alignment has enabled Danone to develop innovative solutions that contribute to its mission and drive long-term success.

Overcoming Barriers to Purpose-Driven Innovation

Despite the benefits of purpose-driven innovation, organizations certain barriers may hinder organizations' efforts. Common challenges include resistance to change, limited resources, and misalignment between purpose and business goals. Leaders should proactively address these barriers to create an environment where purpose-driven innovation can thrive.

Strategies for overcoming barriers include fostering a culture of openness and inclusivity, providing resources and support for innovation, and ensuring alignment between purpose and strategic objectives. Leaders should also communicate the value of purpose-driven innovation to all stakeholders, building buy-in and support.

Addressing barriers to innovation involves creating a supportive environment where employees feel empowered to take risks and explore new ideas. Employee empowerment can involve providing training and development programs, allocating resources for innovation projects, and fostering a culture of collaboration and continuous improvement.

Case Study: Interface

Interface, a global manufacturer of modular flooring, faced significant challenges in its journey toward purpose-driven innovation. The company's purpose "to lead industry to love the world" guided its mission to become a sustainable and restorative enterprise (Interface, n.d.). However, Interface encountered resistance to change and resource constraints as it pursued its sustainability goals.

To overcome these barriers, Interface's leaders fostered a culture of inclusivity and transparency, involving employees at all levels in the company's sustainability initiatives. The company also invested in research and development to develop innovative, sustainable products and processes. By addressing barriers and aligning innovation efforts with its purpose, Interface has achieved significant progress in its sustainability journey and demonstrated the power of purpose-driven innovation.

Interface's approach highlights the importance of engaging employees and stakeholders in the innovation process. By creating a culture of inclusivity and transparency, Interface has been able to overcome challenges and drive meaningful progress toward its sustainability goals.

Measuring the Impact of Purpose-Driven Innovation

Measuring the impact of purpose-driven innovation is essential for demonstrating its value and ensuring accountability. Organizations can use various metrics to assess the success of their innovation efforts and their alignment with the organization's purpose.

KPIs for purpose-driven innovation may include financial metrics, such as revenue growth and return on investment, as well as non-financial metrics, such as environmental impact, social impact, and customer satisfaction. Regularly reviewing and reporting on these metrics can provide insights into the effectiveness of innovation initiatives and help identify areas for improvement.

Organizations can use sustainability reports, impact assessments, and dashboards to track and communicate the performance of their innovation efforts. Transparent reporting helps build trust with stakeholders and demonstrates the organization's commitment to its purpose.

Case Study: Novo Nordisk

Novo Nordisk, a global healthcare company, measures the impact of its purpose-driven innovation through its "Triple Bottom Line" approach, which evaluates performance based on financial, social, and environmental criteria. The company's purpose "to drive change to defeat diabetes and other serious chronic diseases" guides its innovation efforts and impact assessment (Novo Nordisk, n.d.).

The company's KPIs include measures of patient outcomes, access to healthcare, and environmental sustainability. By regularly reviewing and reporting on these metrics, Novo Nordisk demonstrates the value of its purpose-driven innovation and ensures accountability. This holistic approach has enhanced Novo Nordisk's reputation and driven its success in the healthcare industry.

Novo Nordisk's comprehensive approach to measuring the impact of its innovation efforts highlights the importance of using a balanced set of metrics that reflect the organization's purpose and long-term goals. This transparency and accountability help build trust with stakeholders and drive continuous improvement.

Conclusion

Purpose-driven innovation is a powerful strategy for creating value that extends beyond financial returns. By aligning innovation efforts with the organization's purpose, leaders can inspire creativity, drive growth, and make a positive impact on society and the environment. Through real-world examples and practical strategies, this chapter has highlighted the critical role of purpose-driven innovation in transforming organizations and achieving long-term success. By fostering a culture of innovation, leveraging technology, collaborating with partners, and measuring impact, leaders can ensure that their organizations thrive and contribute to a better world.

References

3M. (n.d.). About 3M. https://www.3m.com/3M/en_US/company-us/

Apple. (n.d.). About Apple. https://www.apple.com/about/

Christensen, C. M. (1997). The innovator's dilemma: When new technologies cause great firms to fail. Harvard Business School Press.

Christensen, C. M. (2016). Competing against luck: The story of innovation and customer choice. HarperBusiness.

Danone. (n.d.). Our mission. https://www.danone.com/about-danone/our-mission.html

Ellen MacArthur Foundation. (n.d.). About us. https://www.ellenmacarthurfoundation.org/about

Google X. (n.d.). About Google X. https://x.company/about/

IBM. (n.d.). Our purpose. https://www.ibm.com/ibm/us/en/

Interface. (n.d.). Mission statement. https://www.interface.com/US/en-US/sustainability/mission-statement.html

Novo Nordisk. (n.d.). About us. https://www.novonordisk.com/about.html

Tesla. (n.d.). About Tesla. https://www.tesla.com/about

Unilever. (n.d.). Sustainable Living. https://www.unilever.com/sustainable-living/

CHAPTER 8

Purpose in Crisis Management

Introduction

Crisis management is an inevitable aspect of organizational leadership. Whether it is a financial downturn, a natural disaster, a public relations debacle, or a global pandemic, crises test the resilience and adaptability of organizations. However, a clear and compelling purpose can serve as a guiding star during these turbulent times, helping leaders make decisions that are aligned with the organization's values and long-term goals. This chapter explores the role of purpose in crisis management, detailing how organizations can leverage their purpose to navigate crises effectively, maintain trust, and emerge stronger. Through theoretical insights and real-world examples, we will understand the critical importance of purpose in steering organizations through adversity.

The Nature of Crises and Their Impact on Organizations

Crises are disruptive events that threaten to harm an organization or its stakeholders. They can arise from various sources, including internal issues such as operational failures and external factors such as economic recessions or natural disasters. The impact of a crisis can be widespread, affecting an organization's financial stability, reputation, employee morale, and customer trust.

The immediate response to a crisis often focuses on mitigating damage and restoring normalcy. However, how an organization manages a crisis can have long-term implications. Effective crisis management involves not only addressing the immediate threat but also leveraging the crisis as an opportunity to reinforce the organization's purpose, build resilience, and enhance stakeholder relationships.

Crises require swift and decisive action. However, the nature of crises often involves significant uncertainty and complexity. Hence, navigating it effectively can be challenging for leaders. Understanding the multifaceted impacts of crises and the ways in which they can influence an organization helps leaders prepare better and respond more effectively when such events occur.

The Role of Purpose in Crisis Management

A well-defined purpose provides a stable foundation that guides decision-making and actions during a crisis. It ensures that the organization's response aligns with its core values and long-term vision, maintaining consistency and integrity even under pressure. Purpose-driven crisis management involves using the organization's purpose as a compass to navigate uncertainty by making decisions that reflect the organization's commitment to its stakeholders and societal responsibilities.

Purpose also helps maintain focus and clarity during a crisis. When the situation is chaotic and the stakes are high, a clear purpose can cut through the noise, providing a sense of direction and priority. Purpose enables leaders to communicate effectively with stakeholders, ensuring that their actions are understood and supported.

During a crisis, leaders often face tough choices that can have significant consequences on the organization. A clear purpose helps prioritize these choices by providing a framework for evaluating options and their alignment with the organization's values. This clarity is essential for maintaining stakeholder trust and organizational cohesion during turbulent times.

Case Study: Johnson & Johnson and the Tylenol Crisis

One of the most cited examples of purpose-driven crisis management is Johnson & Johnson's handling of the Tylenol crisis in 1982. When cyanide-laced Tylenol capsules led to several deaths, Johnson & Johnson faced a severe public health crisis. Guided by its Credo, which emphasizes putting the needs and well-being of the people it serves first, the company made a bold decision to recall 31 million bottles of Tylenol despite the significant financial cost (Johnson & Johnson, n.d.).

Johnson & Johnson's response was guided by its purpose of caring for its customers and maintaining trust. The company's transparent communication, decisive actions, and commitment to safety restored public confidence and set a new standard for crisis management in the pharmaceutical industry. By aligning its response with its purpose, Johnson & Johnson not only mitigated the immediate crisis but also strengthened its reputation and trust with stakeholders.

The Tylenol crisis also highlighted the importance of preparedness and having clear protocols that are aligned with organizational purpose. Johnson & Johnson's ability to act swiftly and decisively was underpinned by its strong sense of purpose and commitment to ethical behavior, demonstrating the power of purpose-driven leadership in crises.

Building a Crisis-Ready Culture

Preparing for a crisis involves building a culture that prioritizes resilience, adaptability, and ethical decision-making. Leaders play a critical role in fostering this culture by embedding the organization's purpose into its crisis management strategies and practices. This approach involves regular training, scenario planning, and establishing clear protocols that align with the organization's values.

A crisis-ready culture is characterized by openness, transparency, and a commitment to continuous improvement. Employees should feel empowered to raise concerns, suggest improvements, and take proactive steps to prevent and mitigate crises. Leaders should model these behaviors, demonstrating a commitment to learning and growth.

Developing a crisis-ready culture requires regular drills and simulations to prepare employees for potential crises. These exercises help identify weaknesses in the organization's response strategies and provide opportunities for improvement. Fostering a culture of psychological safety where employees feel comfortable voicing potential risks is also crucial for early crisis detection and prevention.

Case Study: Southwest Airlines and Operational Disruptions

Southwest Airlines' purpose "to connect people to what's important in their lives through friendly, reliable, and low-cost air travel" guides its approach to crisis management (Southwest Airlines, n.d.). When operational disruptions occur, such as weather-related delays or mechanical issues, Southwest prioritizes transparent communication and customer service.

The company's leaders empower employees to make decisions that reflect its purpose, ensuring that customer needs are met even during disruptions. This crisis-ready culture has helped Southwest maintain high levels of customer satisfaction and loyalty, demonstrating the power of purpose-driven crisis management.

Southwest Airlines' approach to operational disruptions includes real-time communication with passengers, providing timely updates and alternative solutions. The airline's focus on maintaining a positive customer experience, even during crises, aligns with its purpose and builds long-term customer loyalty.

The Importance of Transparent Communication

Transparent communication is essential during a crisis. Stakeholders, including employees, customers, investors, and the public, need accurate and timely information to understand the situation and the organization's response. Transparent communication builds trust, reduces uncertainty, and fosters a sense of shared purpose.

Leaders should communicate openly about the nature of the crisis, the actions being taken, and the expected outcomes. Transparent communication includes acknowledging uncertainties and challenges while providing reassurance about the organization's commitment to its purpose and values. Effective communication also involves listening to stakeholders' concerns and feedback demonstrating empathy and responsiveness.

Transparent communication during a crisis helps manage stakeholder expectations and reduces the spread of misinformation. It also reinforces the organization's commitment to ethical behavior and accountability, which are essential components of maintaining trust during challenging times.

Case Study: Airbnb and the COVID-19 Pandemic

The COVID-19 pandemic presented unprecedented challenges for Airbnb as global travel came to a halt. Airbnb's purpose "to create a world where anyone can belong anywhere" guided its response to the crisis (Airbnb, n.d.). The company prioritized transparent communication with its hosts, guests, and employees, providing regular updates and support.

Airbnb's leaders took decisive actions to align with their purpose, including implementing enhanced cleaning protocols, offering flexible cancellation policies, and launching the "Frontline Stays" program to provide housing for healthcare workers. By maintaining transparent communication and staying true to its purpose, Airbnb navigated the crisis effectively and reinforced its commitment to its community.

The company's proactive and transparent response helped maintain trust with its stakeholders and demonstrated its commitment to safety and well-being. This approach not only mitigated the immediate impact of the crisis but also strengthened Airbnb's brand reputation and community relationships.

Leveraging Purpose to Maintain Employee Morale

Crises can take a significant toll on employee morale, leading to stress, uncertainty, and disengagement. A purpose-driven leadership can help maintain and even boost employee morale during challenging times. When employees understand and believe in the organization's purpose, they are more likely to stay engaged and motivated, even in the face of adversity.

Leaders can leverage the organizational purpose to inspire and support employees, providing a sense of meaning and direction. This approach involves recognizing and celebrating employees' contributions, providing resources and support, and fostering a sense of community and solidarity. By aligning their actions with the organization's purpose, leaders can create a supportive environment that empowers employees to navigate crises.

Maintaining open lines of communication with employees, offering mental health resources, and demonstrating empathy are critical strategies for supporting employee morale during crises. Recognizing and rewarding efforts that align with the organization's purpose further reinforces a sense of shared mission and motivation.

Case Study: Starbucks and Racial Bias Training

In 2018, Starbucks faced a public relations crisis following an incident of racial bias at one of its stores. In response, Starbucks closed over 8,000 stores for a day to conduct racial bias training for its employees. This decision aligned with Starbucks' purpose "to inspire and nurture the human spirit – one person, one cup, and one neighborhood at a time" (Starbucks, n.d.).

Starbucks' leaders used the crisis as an opportunity to reinforce the company's commitment to diversity and inclusion, providing employees with the training and resources needed to address bias and foster an inclusive environment. This purpose-driven response helped rebuild Starbucks' trust with customers and employees, demonstrating the company's commitment to its values.

The company's proactive approach to addressing the incident and investing in employee training highlighted its dedication to creating an inclusive and respectful environment. This action not only addressed the immediate issue but also strengthened Starbucks' long-term commitment to its purpose and values.

Adapting and Innovating During a Crisis

Crises often require organizations to adapt and innovate to survive and thrive. A clear purpose can guide these efforts, ensuring that innovations are aligned with the organization's values and long-term goals. Purpose-driven innovation during a crisis involves identifying new opportunities, developing creative solutions, and leveraging existing strengths to address emerging challenges.

Leaders should foster a culture of agility and experimentation, encouraging employees to think creatively and take calculated risks. This strategy involves providing the resources and support needed to innovate, as well as recognizing and rewarding innovative efforts. By aligning innovation with purpose, organizations can navigate crises effectively and emerge stronger.

Adapting to crises can involve adopting novel business models, exploring new markets, or developing new products and services that meet evolving customer needs. Encouraging a culture of continuous improvement and innovation helps organizations remain resilient and responsive during challenging times.

Case Study: Ford and World War II

During World War II, Ford Motor Company faced significant challenges as the automotive industry was disrupted by the war effort. Guided by its purpose "to build great products that contribute to a better world," Ford adapted its operations to support the war effort (Ford, n.d.).

Ford shifted its production from civilian vehicles to military equipment, including airplanes, tanks, and jeeps. This adaptation not only supported the war effort but also demonstrated Ford's commitment to its purpose and values. By leveraging its strengths and aligning its innovation efforts with its purpose, Ford navigated the crisis effectively and emerged as a stronger and more resilient company.

The company's ability to rapidly shift its production and contribute to the war effort showcased its resilience and adaptability. This experience reinforced the importance of having a clear purpose that guides decision-making and innovation during crises.

The Role of Corporate Social Responsibility in Crisis Management

Corporate Social Responsibility (CSR) plays a crucial role in purpose-driven crisis management. Organizations with a strong commitment to CSR are better positioned to respond to crises in ways that reflect their values and contribute positively to society. CSR initiatives can enhance an organization's reputation, build trust with stakeholders, and create a sense of shared purpose.

During a crisis, organizations can leverage their CSR efforts to support affected communities, provide resources and assistance, and demonstrate their commitment to social and environmental responsibility. To perform this function, CSR initiatives must be aligned with the organization's purpose, and actions must be transparent, ethical, and impactful.

CSR initiatives during crises can include providing financial support to affected communities, donating products or services, and engaging in volunteer efforts. Demonstrating a commitment to social responsibility helps organizations build stronger relationships with stakeholders and enhances their long-term resilience.

Case Study: Cisco and Disaster Response

Cisco's purpose "to power an inclusive future for all" guides its CSR efforts, including its response to natural disasters and humanitarian crises (Cisco, n.d.). The company's "Tactical Operations" team provides emergency communications and technology support to disaster-stricken areas, helping restore connectivity and support relief efforts.

During the COVID-19 pandemic, Cisco leveraged its technology and resources to support remote work and online education, providing free access to its Webex platform and other tools. By aligning its CSR initiatives with its purpose, Cisco demonstrated its commitment to social responsibility and made a positive impact during the crisis.

Cisco's proactive approach to disaster response and support for remote work and education during the pandemic reinforced its purpose and strengthened its relationships with stakeholders. These efforts highlighted the company's commitment to using technology for social good and supporting communities in times of need.

Learning and Growing from a Crisis

Crises provide valuable opportunities for learning and growth. Purpose-driven organizations use crises as a catalyst for continuous improvement by reflecting on their experiences, identifying lessons learned, and making necessary adjustments to enhance their resilience and preparedness. This approach involves conducting thorough post-crisis reviews, gathering feedback from stakeholders, and implementing changes to policies, practices, and strategies.

Leaders should foster a culture of continuous learning, encouraging employees to share insights and suggestions for improvement. By integrating these lessons into the organization's operations, leaders can strengthen their crisis management capabilities and ensure that the organization is better prepared for future challenges.

Learning from crises involves analyzing what worked well and what did not, identifying gaps in response strategies, and developing action plans to address these gaps. Creating a repository of best practices and lessons learned helps organizations build institutional knowledge and improve their crisis management processes.

Case Study: Toyota and the Recalls Crisis

In 2009–2010, Toyota faced a significant crisis involving large-scale recalls due to safety issues. Guided by its purpose "to produce happiness for all" and its commitment to quality and safety, Toyota conducted a thorough review of its processes and implemented comprehensive changes to address these issues (Toyota, n.d.).

Toyota's leaders prioritized transparency, communication, and continuous improvement, enhancing the company's quality control measures and restoring public trust. By learning from the crisis and aligning its response with its purpose, Toyota strengthened its operations and reaffirmed its commitment to safety and customer satisfaction.

Toyota's comprehensive review and improvements to its quality control processes highlighted the company's commitment to continuous learning and excellence. This proactive approach not only helped address the immediate issues but also strengthened Toyota's long-term resilience and reputation for quality.

Sustaining Purpose-Driven Crisis Management

Sustaining purpose-driven crisis management requires ongoing commitment and effort from leaders. This process involves regularly revisiting and reaffirming the organization's purpose, integrating purpose into crisis management plans and protocols, and fostering a culture of resilience and ethical decision-making.

Leaders should ensure that purpose-driven crisis management is embedded into the organization's strategic planning, risk management, and performance evaluation processes. This alignment ensures that the organization remains focused on its long-term goals and values, even in the face of adversity.

Embedding purpose-driven crisis management into organizational processes includes developing crisis response plans that align with the organization's purpose, conducting regular risk assessments, and integrating crisis management into employee training programs.

Case Study: Patagonia and Environmental Advocacy

Patagonia's commitment to its purpose "to save our home planet," guides its crisis management efforts, particularly in response to environmental challenges (Patagonia, n.d.). The company's leaders prioritize environmental advocacy, using crises as opportunities to raise awareness and drive positive change.

For example, Patagonia's response to the Trump administration's reduction of protected lands in Bears Ears National Monument involved a high-profile advocacy campaign and legal action to restore protections. By aligning its crisis response with its purpose, Patagonia demonstrated its commitment to environmental stewardship and mobilized its stakeholders to support the cause.

Patagonia's proactive advocacy and legal efforts highlighted the company's dedication to its purpose and environmental sustainability. These actions not only addressed the immediate crisis but also reinforced Patagonia's long-term commitment to protecting the environment and driving positive change.

Conclusion

Purpose-driven crisis management is essential for navigating uncertainty, maintaining trust, and emerging stronger from adversity. A clear and compelling purpose provides a stable foundation that guides decision-making, inspires employees, and fosters resilience. Through real-world examples and practical strategies, this chapter has highlighted the critical role of purpose in crisis management. By building a crisis-ready culture, maintaining transparent communication, leveraging CSR initiatives, and fostering continuous learning, leaders can ensure that their organizations thrive and make a positive impact during and after crises.

References

Airbnb. (n.d.). About Us. https://www.airbnb.com/about

Cisco. (n.d.). Corporate Social Responsibility. https://www.cisco.com/c/en/us/about/csr.html

Ford. (n.d.). Our Purpose. https://corporate.ford.com/company.html

Johnson & Johnson. (n.d.). Our Credo. https://www.jnj.com/credo/

Patagonia. (n.d.). Mission Statement. https://www.patagonia.com/mission-statement/

Southwest Airlines. (n.d.). About Southwest Airlines. https://www.southwest.com/html/about-southwest/

Starbucks. (n.d.). Our Mission and Values. https://www.starbucks.com/about-us/company-information/mission-statement

CHAPTER 9

Building Sustainable Success through Aligned Purpose

Introduction

Sustainable success in the business world is achieved not merely through short-term profits but by creating long-term value that benefits all stakeholders. Aligned purpose is a crucial element in achieving this sustainable success. Organizations that embed their purpose into every aspect of their operations are better equipped to navigate challenges, foster innovation, and build resilience. This chapter explores the strategies for building sustainable success through aligned purpose, highlighting the importance of strategic alignment, stakeholder engagement, and continuous improvement. Through theoretical insights and real-world examples, we will understand how aligned purpose can drive long-term success and make a positive impact on society.

The Concept of Sustainable Success

Sustainable success refers to the ability of an organization to achieve its goals consistently over time while creating value for all stakeholders. This concept goes beyond financial performance to include social, environmental, and ethical dimensions. Sustainable success is characterized by resilience, adaptability, and a commitment to continuous improvement.

Aligned purpose is central to sustainable success. The alignment of an organization's purpose with its strategy, operations, and culture creates a unified direction that drives performance and engagement. Purpose-driven organizations are better able to attract and retain talent, build strong relationships with customers and partners, and navigate complex challenges.

Strategic Alignment and Purpose

Strategic alignment involves ensuring that the organization's goals, strategies, and actions are consistent with its purpose. This alignment creates a clear roadmap for achieving long-term success by guiding decision-making and resource allocation.

Because leaders play a critical role in achieving strategic alignment, they must articulate a clear and compelling purpose, communicate it consistently, and integrate it into the organization's strategic planning processes. This approach involves setting purpose-driven goals, developing strategies that align with the organization's values, and regularly reviewing and adjusting plans based on feedback and changing circumstances.

For example, strategic alignment can include defining long-term sustainability goals that align with the organization's purpose, such as reducing carbon emissions or improving community health. Regular strategic reviews ensure that these goals remain relevant and that progress is tracked and reported transparently.

Case Study: IKEA

IKEA's purpose "to create a better everyday life for the many people" guides its strategic alignment and long-term success (IKEA, n.d.). This purpose is reflected in its business model, product design, and sustainability initiatives. The company's strategic alignment involves setting ambitious goals for affordability, quality, and sustainability.

IKEA's "People & Planet Positive" strategy outlines its commitment to sustainability, including goals for renewable energy, sustainable sourcing, and circular economy practices. By aligning its strategies with its purpose, IKEA has built a resilient and innovative business model that delivers long-term value to customers, employees, and the environment.

Engaging Stakeholders in Purpose-Driven Success

Stakeholder engagement is essential for building sustainable success through an aligned purpose. Engaging stakeholders—including employees, customers, suppliers, investors, and communities—ensures that their needs and perspectives are considered in the organization's decision-making processes.

Effective stakeholder engagement involves open communication, active listening, and collaboration. Leaders should create opportunities for stakeholders to provide input and feedback and demonstrate a commitment to addressing their concerns. This engagement fosters trust, loyalty, and a sense of shared purpose.

Engaging stakeholders can involve conducting regular surveys to gather feedback, hosting town hall meetings to discuss initiatives, and creating advisory boards that include stakeholder representatives. Transparent communication about how stakeholder input is used to guide decisions helps build trust and commitment.

Case Study: Unilever

Unilever's purpose "to make sustainable living commonplace" guides its stakeholder engagement efforts (Unilever, n.d.). The company actively engages with a diverse range of stakeholders, including consumers, suppliers, NGOs, and policymakers, to drive its sustainability agenda.

Unilever's "Sustainable Living Plan" includes initiatives to improve people's health and well-being, reduce environmental impact, and enhance livelihoods. By collaborating with stakeholders, Unilever has developed innovative solutions that address global challenges and create shared value. This engagement has strengthened Unilever's reputation and contributed to its sustainable success.

Fostering a Culture of Continuous Improvement

Continuous improvement is a key component of sustainable success. Purpose-driven organizations are committed to learning, innovation, and adaptability. This commitment involves regularly assessing performance, identifying areas for improvement, and implementing changes that align with the organization's purpose and goals.

Leaders should foster a culture that values continuous improvement, encouraging employees to seek out new ideas and opportunities for growth. This culture can be created by providing resources and support for professional development, recognizing and rewarding innovative efforts, and promoting a mindset of curiosity and experimentation.

Creating a culture of continuous improvement can involve implementing lean management practices, using performance metrics to identify areas for improvement, and fostering an environment where employees feel safe to experiment and learn from past failures.

Case Study: Toyota

Toyota's commitment to continuous improvement, known as "kaizen," is integral to its purpose "to produce happiness for all" (Toyota, n.d.). The kaizen philosophy encourages employees at all levels to identify and implement improvements, fostering a culture of innovation and excellence.

Toyota's "Toyota Production System" (TPS) exemplifies this commitment to continuous improvement. The TPS focuses on eliminating waste, optimizing processes, and enhancing quality. By aligning its continuous improvement efforts with its purpose, Toyota has built a resilient and adaptable organization that consistently delivers high-quality products and services.

Leveraging Technology for Sustainable Success

Technology plays a crucial role in achieving sustainable success through aligned purposes. Advances in digital technologies, such as artificial intelligence (AI), blockchain, and the Internet of Things (IoT), provide new opportunities for organizations to enhance their operations, innovate, and create value.

Leaders should stay informed about emerging technologies and explore how they can be applied to achieve the organization's purpose.

This goal requires investing in research and development, collaborating with technology partners, and fostering a culture of digital literacy and experimentation.

Leveraging technology can involve using AI for predictive analytics to improve decision-making, implementing blockchain for supply chain transparency, and using IoT for monitoring and reducing environmental impact.

Case Study: IBM

IBM's purpose "to be essential to our clients, to the world, and to each other" guides its use of technology to drive sustainable success (IBM, n.d.). IBM leverages advanced technologies to develop innovative solutions that address complex challenges and create positive social and environmental impact.

For example, IBM's "Watson" AI platform has been used to develop solutions in healthcare, environmental management, and disaster response. IBM's "Blockchain for Good" initiative leverages blockchain technology to enhance transparency and accountability in supply chains, supporting ethical sourcing and reducing fraud. By aligning its technological innovations with its purpose, IBM has created solutions that deliver significant value and contribute to sustainable success.

Aligning Purpose with Environmental Sustainability

Environmental sustainability is a critical component of sustainable success. Purpose-driven organizations recognize their responsibility to minimize their environmental impact and contribute to the health of the planet. This responsibility involves setting ambitious sustainability goals, implementing environmentally friendly practices, and engaging stakeholders in sustainability initiatives.

Leaders should integrate environmental sustainability into the organization's strategic planning and operations. This responsibility requires conducting environmental impact assessments, developing sustainability strategies, and regularly reviewing and reporting on progress. By aligning purpose with environmental sustainability, organizations can create long-term value and contribute to global sustainability efforts. Implementing environmental sustainability can include adopting renewable energy, reducing waste through circular economy practices, and investing in sustainable product development.

Case Study: Patagonia

Patagonia's purpose, "to save our home planet," guides its commitment to environmental sustainability (Patagonia, n.d.). The company's sustainability initiatives include using recycled materials, reducing carbon emissions, and promoting environmental activism.

Patagonia's "Worn Wear" program encourages customers to repair and reuse their products, reducing waste and promoting a circular economy. The company also engages in environmental advocacy, supporting initiatives to protect public lands and combat climate change. By aligning its purpose with environmental sustainability, Patagonia has built a strong brand reputation and created long-term value for its stakeholders.

The Role of Ethical Leadership in Sustainable Success

Ethical leadership is fundamental to achieving sustainable success through an aligned purpose. Ethical leaders prioritize integrity, transparency, and fairness in their decision-making and actions. They model ethical behavior, hold themselves and others accountable to high ethical standards, and create a culture of trust and respect.

Ethical leadership involves making decisions that consider the long-term impact on all stakeholders rather than focusing solely on short-term gains. This obligation includes addressing ethical dilemmas, promoting diversity and inclusion, and ensuring that the organization's operations align with its values.

Ethical leadership can be demonstrated through transparent reporting practices, ethical sourcing policies, and fostering a culture where ethical behavior is rewarded and unethical behavior is addressed.

Case Study: Salesforce

Salesforce's purpose "to empower companies to connect with their customers in a whole new way" guides its commitment to ethical leadership and social responsibility (Salesforce, n.d.). The company's leaders prioritize transparency, accountability, and inclusivity in their decision-making processes.

The company's "1-1-1" philanthropic model dedicates 1% of the company's equity, 1% of its product, and 1% of employees' time to philanthropic initiatives. This commitment to giving back aligns with Salesforce's purpose and creates a positive impact on society. By prioritizing ethical leadership, Salesforce has built a strong reputation and achieved sustainable success.

Engaging Employees in Purpose-Driven Success

Employee engagement is critical for achieving sustainable success through an aligned purpose. Engaged employees are more likely to be motivated, productive, and committed to the organization's goals. Purpose-driven organizations create a work environment where employees feel valued, supported, and connected to the organization's mission.

Leaders can engage employees by clearly communicating the organization's purpose, providing opportunities for professional development, and recognizing and rewarding contributions. These roles require fostering a culture of collaboration, inclusivity, and continuous learning.

Engaging employees can involve initiatives such as regular town hall meetings, purpose-driven team-building activities, and creating career development plans that align with the organization's values.

Case Study: Zappos

Zappos' purpose "to deliver happiness to customers, employees, and vendors" guides its approach to employee engagement (Zappos, n.d.). The company's leaders prioritize creating a positive and supportive work environment where employees feel empowered to contribute to the company's mission.

The company's unique onboarding process, which includes a culture fit interview and a $2,000 offer to quit, ensures that new hires are aligned with the company's values. The company also provides opportunities for professional development and recognizes employees' contributions through its "Hero Awards" program. By engaging employees and aligning their efforts with its purpose, Zappos has built a strong culture and achieved sustainable success.

Measuring and Reporting on Sustainable Success

Measuring and reporting on sustainable success are essential for demonstrating the value of aligned purpose and ensuring accountability. Organizations can use various metrics to assess their performance and impact, including financial, social, and environmental indicators.

Key performance indicators (KPIs) for sustainable success may include revenue growth, customer satisfaction, employee engagement, environmental impact, and social contributions. Regularly reviewing and reporting on these metrics provides insights into the organization's progress and identifies areas for improvement.

Organizations can use sustainability reports, impact assessments, and dashboards to track and communicate their performance. Transparency in reporting helps build trust with stakeholders and demonstrates the organization's commitment to its purpose.

Case Study: Novo Nordisk

Novo Nordisk, a global healthcare company, measures its sustainable success through its "Triple Bottom Line" approach, which involves evaluating performance based on financial, social, and environmental criteria. The company's purpose "to drive change to defeat diabetes and other serious chronic diseases" guides its impact assessment and reporting (Novo Nordisk, n.d.).

The company's KPIs include measures of patient outcomes, access to healthcare, and environmental sustainability. By regularly reviewing and reporting on these metrics, the company demonstrates the value of its purpose-driven efforts and ensures accountability. This holistic approach has enhanced Novo Nordisk's reputation and driven its success in the healthcare industry.

Building Resilient and Adaptable Organizations

Resilience and adaptability are critical components of sustainable success. Purpose-driven organizations are better equipped to navigate uncertainty, respond to change, and recover from setbacks. Building resilience and adaptability requires fostering a culture of agility, continuous learning, and innovation.

Leaders should create an environment where employees feel empowered to take risks, experiment, and learn from failure. This responsibility involves providing the resources and support needed to adapt to changing circumstances and encouraging a mindset of resilience and adaptability.

Building resilient organizations can include implementing robust risk management practices, developing contingency plans, and fostering a culture where flexibility and innovation are encouraged.

Case Study: Netflix

Netflix's purpose, "to entertain the world," guides its approach to resilience and adaptability (Netflix, n.d.). The company's leaders prioritize innovation and continuous improvement, enabling Netflix to navigate industry disruptions and maintain its competitive edge.

The company's strategic pivot from a DVD rental service to a global streaming platform exemplifies its adaptability. Netflix's focus on data-driven decision-making, content personalization, and original programming has driven its growth and success. By aligning its purpose with a culture of resilience and adaptability, Netflix has built a strong and sustainable business model.

Conclusion

Building sustainable success through aligned purpose requires a holistic approach that integrates purpose into every aspect of the organization's operations. By achieving strategic alignment, engaging stakeholders, fostering continuous improvement, leveraging technology, and promoting ethical leadership, organizations can create long-term value and make a positive impact on society. Through real-world examples and practical strategies, this chapter has highlighted the critical role of aligned purpose in driving sustainable success. By prioritizing purpose-driven success, leaders can ensure that their organizations thrive and contribute to a better world.

References

IBM. (n.d.). Our purpose. https://www.ibm.com/ibm/us/en/

IKEA. (n.d.). People & Planet Positive. https://www.ikea.com/ms/en_JP/about_ikea/people_and_planet/

Netflix. (n.d.). About Netflix. https://jobs.netflix.com/mission

Novo Nordisk. (n.d.). About us. https://www.novonordisk.com/about.html

Patagonia. (n.d.). Mission Statement. https://www.patagonia.com/mission-statement/

Salesforce. (n.d.). Equality. https://www.salesforce.com/company/equality/

Toyota. (n.d.). Toyota Global Vision. https://global.toyota/en/company/vision-and-philosophy/

Unilever. (n.d.). Sustainable Living. https://www.unilever.com/sustainable-living/

Zappos. (n.d.). Delivering Happiness. https://www.zappos.com/about/delivering-happiness

CHAPTER 10

The Future of Aligned Leadership

Introduction

As the business landscape continues to evolve, the role of aligned leadership becomes increasingly critical. Leaders who effectively align their organization's purpose with its strategy, operations, and culture can drive sustainable success and make a significant positive impact on society. This chapter explores the future of aligned leadership by examining emerging trends, challenges, and opportunities. By understanding the evolving expectations of stakeholders, leveraging new technologies, and fostering a culture of continuous learning, leaders can navigate the complexities of the future and ensure their organizations thrive.

The Evolving Expectations of Stakeholders

Stakeholders, including employees, customers, investors, and communities, are increasingly demanding that organizations demonstrate a commitment to ethical behavior, social responsibility, and sustainability. These evolving expectations require leaders to align their organization's purpose with stakeholder needs and priorities, fostering trust and loyalty.

Employees

Employees today seek meaningful work and desire to be part of organizations that are aligned with their values. They prioritize organizations that offer opportunities for professional growth, inclusivity, and a positive work environment. Leaders should create a purpose-driven culture that engages employees, fosters collaboration, and supports their well-being.

To meet these expectations, leaders should focus on creating opportunities for employees to connect with the organization's purpose. They can achieve this goal through regular communications about how their work contributes to the organization's goals, recognition programs that celebrate purpose-driven achievements, and development programs that help employees grow in alignment with the organization's values.

Customers

Customers are becoming more conscious of the social and environmental impact of their purchasing decisions. They favor brands that demonstrate a commitment to sustainability, ethical sourcing, and social responsibility. Leaders should ensure that their organization's purpose is reflected in its products, services, and customer interactions.

To be aligned with customer expectations, an organization should integrate its purpose into its brand messaging and customer experiences. This integration can be achieved through transparent marketing practices, sustainable product development, and initiatives that engage customers in the organization's social and environmental efforts. Providing platforms for customer feedback and involving them in co-creating solutions can also deepen their connection to the brand's purpose.

Investors

Investors are increasingly incorporating environmental, social, and governance (ESG) criteria into their investment decisions. They seek organizations that manage risks effectively, demonstrate long-term resilience, and contribute positively to society. Leaders should communicate their organization's purpose and impact clearly to attract and retain purpose-driven investors.

Organizations can attract purpose-driven investors by integrating the ESG criteria into their strategic planning and reporting. This integration can be achieved by setting measurable sustainability goals, regularly reporting on progress, and engaging with investors to understand their expectations and concerns. Transparency and accountability are key to building investor trust and demonstrating the alignment between purpose and performance.

Communities

Communities expect organizations to contribute to their well-being and address social and environmental challenges. Leaders should engage with communities, understand their needs, and collaborate on initiatives that create shared value. By aligning their organization's purpose with community priorities, leaders can build strong relationships and enhance their organization's reputation.

Effective community engagement involves partnering with local organizations, participating in community development projects, and creating programs that address specific community needs. Leaders should ensure that community engagement efforts are genuine and aligned with the organization's purpose rather than being seen as superficial or self-serving.

Case Study: BlackRock

BlackRock, one of the world's largest asset management firms, has emphasized the importance of aligning corporate purpose with stakeholder expectations. In his annual letters to CEOs, BlackRock CEO Larry Fink calls for companies to focus on purpose and long-term value creation. BlackRock has integrated the ESG criteria into its investment processes and actively engages with companies on sustainability issues (BlackRock, n.d.).

By aligning its purpose with evolving stakeholder expectations, BlackRock has positioned itself as a leader in responsible investing and has driven positive change in the business community. The firm's commitment to the ESG criteria has not only attracted purpose-driven investors but also influenced the broader corporate landscape, encouraging other companies to adopt similar practices.

Leveraging New Technologies for Aligned Leadership

Technological advancements are transforming the way organizations operate and interact with stakeholders. Leaders should leverage new technologies to enhance their organization's purpose-driven efforts, drive innovation, and improve stakeholder engagement.

Digital Transformation

Digital transformation involves integrating digital technologies into all aspects of an organization's operations, leading to improved efficiency, innovation, and customer experiences. Leaders should align their digital transformation initiatives with their organization's purpose, ensuring that technology enhances their mission and values.

For example, digital tools can be used to streamline processes, improve data analytics, and enhance customer engagement. By aligning these initiatives with the organization's purpose, leaders can ensure that technology serves as a catalyst for achieving long-term goals and creating value for stakeholders.

Artificial Intelligence and Data Analytics

Artificial intelligence (AI) and data analytics provide powerful tools for understanding stakeholder needs, optimizing operations, and making informed decisions. Leaders can use AI and data analytics to align their organization's efforts with its purpose by identifying opportunities for sustainability, improving customer experiences, and enhancing employee engagement.

AI can help organizations analyze vast amounts of data to uncover patterns and insights that inform strategic decisions. For example, predictive analytics can be used to anticipate customer needs and preferences, allowing organizations to tailor their products and services to their purpose and customer expectations.

Blockchain Technology

Blockchain technology offers transparency, security, and accountability in transactions and supply chains. Leaders can leverage blockchain to support ethical sourcing, traceability, and fair trade practices, aligning their organization's operations with its purpose and values.

For instance, blockchain can be used to verify the authenticity of products and ensure that they are sourced ethically and sustainably. This transparency builds trust with stakeholders and reinforces the organization's commitment to its purpose.

Case Study: Microsoft's AI for Good

Microsoft's AI for Good initiative exemplifies the use of advanced technologies to drive purpose-driven efforts. Microsoft leverages AI to address global challenges in healthcare, environmental sustainability, and accessibility. The initiative aligns with Microsoft's purpose "to empower every person and every organization on the planet to achieve more" (Microsoft, n.d.).

Projects under AI for Good include using AI to predict and prevent diseases, monitor environmental changes, and develop assistive technologies for people with disabilities. By aligning its technological innovations with its purpose, Microsoft has created a significant positive impact and demonstrated the potential of AI for social good.

Fostering a Culture of Continuous Learning

In a rapidly changing world, continuous learning is essential for aligned leadership. Leaders should foster a culture that values curiosity, innovation, and adaptability, enabling their organizations to navigate complexity and seize new opportunities.

Lifelong Learning

Lifelong learning involves encouraging employees to continuously develop their skills and knowledge. Leaders can support lifelong learning by providing access to training, development programs, and educational resources. By aligning learning initiatives with the organization's purpose, leaders can ensure that employees are equipped to contribute to the organization's goals and adapt to changing circumstances.

Organizations can create personalized learning paths for employees, offering a mix of online courses, workshops, and mentorship opportunities. Encouraging employees to pursue certifications and advanced degrees can also enhance their skills and align their growth with the organization's purpose.

Collaboration and Knowledge Sharing

Collaboration and knowledge sharing are critical for fostering innovation and continuous improvement. Leaders should create an environment that encourages open communication, cross-functional collaboration, and the sharing of best practices. By promoting a culture of collaboration, leaders can harness diverse perspectives and drive purpose-driven innovation.

This goal can be achieved using collaborative tools and platforms that facilitate information sharing and teamwork. Regular cross-departmental meetings, innovation workshops, and collaborative projects can also help break down silos and encourage the exchange of ideas.

Feedback and Reflection

Regular feedback and reflection are essential for continuous learning and growth. Leaders should implement mechanisms for gathering feedback from employees, customers, and other stakeholders and use this feedback to inform decision-making and improve performance. Reflecting on successes and challenges helps organizations learn from their experiences and continuously align their efforts with their purpose.

Organizations can use surveys, focus groups, and one-on-one meetings to gather feedback and identify areas for improvement. Encouraging a culture of constructive feedback and continuous reflection helps both employees and leaders to grow and develop.

Case Study: Google's Learning Culture

Google's commitment to continuous learning is reflected in its purpose "to organize the world's information and make it universally accessible and useful" (Google, n.d.). The company fosters a learning culture through initiatives such as "20% time," where employees can spend 20% of their work time on projects they are passionate about.

Google also offers extensive training and development programs, encouraging employees to pursue new skills and knowledge. The company promotes collaboration and knowledge sharing through internal platforms and events. By fostering a culture of continuous learning, Google has driven innovation and maintained its competitive edge.

Navigating Complexity and Change

The future of aligned leadership requires the ability to navigate complexity and change. Leaders should be adaptable, resilient, and proactive in addressing emerging challenges and opportunities.

Scenario Planning

Scenario planning involves exploring different potential futures and developing strategies to address them. Leaders can use scenario planning to anticipate changes in the business environment, assess risks, and identify opportunities. By aligning scenario planning with their organization's purpose, leaders can ensure that their strategies remain consistent with their values and long-term goals.

Scenario planning exercises can help organizations prepare for various contingencies, from economic downturns to technological disruptions. By considering a range of scenarios, leaders can develop robust strategies that are flexible and adaptable.

Agility and Flexibility

Agility and flexibility are essential for responding to change and uncertainty. Leaders should aim to create agile organizations that can quickly adapt to new circumstances and pivot as needed. Organizational agility can be achieved by fostering a mindset of flexibility, empowering employees to make decisions, and streamlining processes to enable rapid response.

Organizations can adopt agile methodologies, such as Scrum or Kanban, to enhance their ability to respond to changes. Encouraging a culture of experimentation and learning from failure also helps organizations stay agile and innovative.

Resilience Building

Building resilience involves developing the capacity to withstand and recover from disruptions. Leaders can enhance organizational resilience by diversifying revenue streams, investing in risk management, and building strong relationships with stakeholders. By aligning resilience-building efforts with their purpose, leaders can ensure that their organizations remain steadfast in their commitment to their values.

Resilience can be built through robust risk assessment and management practices, as well as through investments in infrastructure and technology that enhance the organization's ability to withstand shocks. Building a resilient workforce through training and support also contributes to overall organizational resilience.

Case Study: Netflix's Adaptability

Netflix's purpose, "to entertain the world," guides its approach to navigating complexity and change (Netflix, n.d.). The company's leaders prioritize agility and adaptability, enabling Netflix to respond to industry disruptions and maintain its competitive edge.

The company's strategic pivot from a DVD rental service to a global streaming platform exemplifies its adaptability. Netflix's focus on data-driven decision-making, content personalization, and original programming has driven its growth and success. By aligning its purpose with a culture of agility and flexibility, Netflix has built a resilient and adaptable organization.

Embracing Diversity and Inclusion

Diversity and inclusion are critical components of aligned leadership. Leaders should create inclusive environments where diverse perspectives are valued, and all employees feel empowered to contribute.

Inclusive Leadership

Inclusive leadership involves actively seeking out and valuing diverse perspectives, creating an environment where everyone feels respected and included. Leaders should model inclusive behaviors, challenge biases, and ensure that decision-making processes are fair and equitable.

Inclusive leaders can implement practices such as blind recruitment, diversity training, and inclusive decision-making processes. They can also create platforms for underrepresented voices to be heard and ensure that diversity and inclusion are integral to the organization's culture.

Diverse Talent Development

Developing diverse talent involves providing opportunities for underrepresented groups to advance and thrive within the organization. Leaders can implement mentorship programs, leadership development initiatives, and inclusive hiring practices to support diverse talent.

Organizations can set diversity targets, offer scholarships and internships for underrepresented groups, and create pathways for career advancement that are accessible to all employees. Providing support networks and resources for diverse employees also helps them succeed.

Inclusive Culture

Creating an inclusive culture involves fostering a sense of belonging and community within the organization. Leaders should promote open communication, celebrate diversity, and address any barriers to inclusion. By aligning their efforts with the organization's purpose, leaders can create a culture that reflects their values and supports sustainable success.

Inclusive cultures can be built through regular diversity and inclusion training, celebrating cultural events, and implementing policies that promote work-life balance and flexibility. Encouraging employee resource groups and diversity councils also help create an inclusive environment.

Case Study: Salesforce's Commitment to Equality

Salesforce's purpose "to empower companies to connect with their customers in a whole new way" guides its commitment to diversity and inclusion (Salesforce, n.d.). The company's leaders prioritize creating an inclusive environment where all employees feel valued and respected.

Salesforce's "Equality" initiatives include regular assessments of pay equity, comprehensive diversity training, and support for employee resource groups. The company's leaders actively promote inclusive behaviors and challenge biases, fostering a culture of equality and inclusion. By embracing diversity and inclusion, Salesforce has built a strong and innovative workforce that drives its success.

The Future of Sustainability and Purpose

As global challenges such as climate change, resource scarcity, and social inequality become more pressing, the future of aligned leadership will increasingly focus on sustainability and purpose. Leaders should integrate sustainability into their strategic planning and operations, ensuring that their organizations contribute positively to the planet and society.

Sustainable Innovation

Sustainable innovation involves developing products, services, and processes that minimize environmental impact and create social value. Leaders can drive sustainable innovation by investing in research and development, collaborating with partners, and fostering a culture of creativity and experimentation.

For example, sustainable innovations can include renewable energy solutions, biodegradable products, and efficient supply chains. By aligning innovation efforts with sustainability goals, organizations can create long-term value and reduce their environmental footprint.

Circular Economy

The circular economy is an economic system that aims to eliminate waste and promote the continuous use of resources. Leaders can embrace circular economy principles by designing products for longevity, implementing closed-loop supply chains, and promoting recycling and reuse.

Organizations can adopt circular economy practices by designing products that are easy to repair, recycle, and up-cycle. They can also develop business models that prioritize resource efficiency and waste reduction, such as product-as-a-service models.

Conclusion

The future of aligned leadership is defined by the ability to navigate complexity, embrace change, and create sustainable success. By aligning their organization's purpose with evolving stakeholder expectations, leveraging new technologies, fostering a culture of continuous learning, and promoting diversity and inclusion, leaders can drive innovation and make a positive impact on society. Through real-world examples and practical strategies, this chapter has highlighted the critical role of aligned leadership in shaping the future of business. By prioritizing purpose-driven leadership, leaders can ensure that their organizations thrive and contribute to a better world.

References

BlackRock. (n.d.). Larry Fink's Annual Letter to CEOs. https://www.blackrock.com/us/individual/larry-fink-ceo-letter

Google. (n.d.). About Google. https://www.google.com/about

Microsoft. (n.d.). AI for Good. https://www.microsoft.com/en-us/ai/ai-for-good

Netflix. (n.d.). About Netflix. https://jobs.netflix.com/mission

Salesforce. (n.d.). Equality. https://www.salesforce.com/company/equality/

www.ingramcontent.com/pod-product-compliance
Lightning Source LLC
Chambersburg PA
CBHW051631120626
46551CB00014B/2030